MP5125

S0-AAK-519

PASSPORT SERIES

Central & South America

Author: Deborah Kopka
Contributors: Nancy Klepper and Ann Edmonds (Brazil)
Editor: Bonnie Krueger
Original Illustrations: Larry Nolte
Design and Layout: Jeff Richards

Printed in the United States of America

ISBN 978-1-4291-2251-1

BRIDGING
the Gaps in Education™
Lorenz Educational Press
P.O. Box 802 • Dayton, OH 45401-0802

for other LEP products visit our website
www.LorenzEducationalPress.com

*All statistics are based on information from 2010.

** For further information on pronunciations, research foreign language dictionaries and/or the Internet.

Metric Conversions

The purpose of this page is to aid in the conversion of measurements in this book from the English system to the metric system. Note that the tables below show two types of ounces. Liquid ounces measure the volume of liquids and have therefore been converted into milliliters. Dry ounces measure weight and have been converted into grams. Because dry substances such as sugar and flour may have different densities, it is advisable to measure them according to weight rather than volume. The measurement unit of the cup has been reserved solely for liquid, or volume, conversions.

Conversion Formulas					
when you know	formula	to find			
		when you know	formula	to find	
teaspoons	× 5	milliliters	× .20	teaspoons	
tablespoons	× 15	milliliters	× .60	tablespoons	
fluid ounces	× 29.57	milliliters	× .03	fluid ounces	
liquid cups	× 240	milliliters	× .004	liquid cups	
U.S. gallons	× 3.78	liters	× .26	U.S. gallons	
dry ounces	× 28.35	grams	× .035	dry ounces	
inches	× 2.54	centimeters	× .39	inches	
square inches	× 6.45	square centimeters	× .15	square inches	
feet	× .30	meters	× 3.28	feet	
square feet	× .09	square meters	× 10.76	square feet	
yards	× .91	meters	× 1.09	yards	
miles	× 1.61	kilometers	× .62	miles	
square miles	× 2.59	square kilometers	× .40	square miles	
Fahrenheit	$(°F - 32) \times \frac{5}{9}$	Celsius	$(°C \times \frac{9}{5}) + 32$	Fahrenheit	

Equivalent Temperatures

32°F = 0°C (water freezes)
212°F = 100°C (water boils)
350°F = 177°C
375°F = 191°C
400°F = 204°C
425°F = 218°C
450°F = 232°C

Common Cooking Conversions

1/2 cup = 120 milliliters
12 fluid ounces = 354.88 milliliters
1 quart (32 ounces) = 950 milliliters
1/2 gallon = 1.89 liters
1 Canadian gallon = 4.55 liters
8 dry ounces (1/2 pound) = 227 grams
16 dry ounces (1 pound) = 454 grams

MP5125

Table of Contents

Argentina

Atacama Desert

CHILE

Antofagasta

PARAGUAY

Gran Chaco

Asunción

Río de la Plata

ARGENTINA

Uruguay R.

Córdoba

Paraná R.

Valparaíso

Mendoza

Andes Mts.

URUGUAY

Buenos Aires ★

★ Montevideo

La Plata

The Pampas

Mar del Plata

Atlantic Ocea

Chiloé Is.

Patagonia

Andes Mts.

N

Stanley

Strait of Magellan

FALKLAND IS.

Tierra de Fuego

Punta Arenas

0	100		300
0	100	300	500 km

Welcome to Argentina!

Very cold and very hot, very high and very low, ancient and modern, Argentina is a land of contrasts. It is the second largest country in South America and the largest in land mass among Spanish-speaking nations. After suffering a financial crisis in 2002 that almost ruined its economy, the country is moving forward again. While some things are changing rapidly, other things, fortunately, remain the same—like its natural beauty and rich cultural heritage!

After you have finished learning about Argentina, be sure to check out page 148 for additional classroom activities.

FAST FACTS

Official Name: Argentine Republic

Location: Southern South America, bordering the South Atlantic Ocean, between Chile and Uruguay

Population: 40,913,584 (2010 estimate)

Capital City: Buenos Aires

Area: 1,068,302 square miles. Argentina is slightly less than three-tenths the size of the U.S.

Major Language: Spanish (the official language)
Italian, German, English, and French

Major Religion: Christianity (predominantly Roman Catholic)

Currency: The peso   1 peso = 100 centavos (cents)

Climate: Mostly temperate. The climate ranges from tropical in the north to subpolar in the south. The hottest and coldest temperatures in South America have been recorded in Argentina.

The Land: Rich plains of the Pampas in the northern half, stretching west to east; the flat to rolling plateaus of Patagonia in the south; the rugged Andes along the western border

Type of Government: Federal presidential republic

Flag:

The Argentine flag has three equal horizontal bands of light blue (at the top), white, and light blue. Centered in the white band is a yellow sun with a human face called the Sun of May. The colors represent the clear skies and snow of the Andes. The sun's features are those of Inti, the Incan sun god. The sun commemorates the appearance of the sun through cloudy skies on May 25, 1810, during the first mass demonstration in favor of independence.

Coat of Arms:

At the top is the Sun of May, which is also found on the Argentine flag. In the center of an ellipse are two shaking hands that come together in friendship, symbolizing the unity of the Argentine provinces. The hands hold a brown pike, which represents the willingness to defend the freedom symbolized by the red Phrygian cap (the traditional French liberty cap) on top of the pike. (In ancient Rome, slaves who had been given their freedom wore the Phrygian cap. These slaves were touched with a wooden pike by their owners before they were freed.) The background in the ellipse is blue on the top half and white on the bottom—the same colors that appear on the Argentine flag. The entire ellipse is surrounded by a laurel wreath, which is a classical symbol of triumph.

National Flower: Ceibo (Cockspur Coral Tree—a flowering tree)

National Animal: Cougar

Motto: "In union and freedom"

Natural Environment

Four Major Regions

Argentina is about 2,400 miles long and about 870 miles wide at its widest point. It lies in the Southern and the Western Hemispheres. Its natural environment makes it truly a land of contrasts, from its subtropical north to its subantarctic south. There are four major regions in the country, and each of them is different. These include:

- the Andes Mountains along the western border with Chile
- the northern plains and Andes foothills
- the central plains of the Pampas where most of the crops are grown
- the flat to rolling southern plateau of Patagonia (including Tierra del Fuego), which is rich in oil

The Andes

South America's major landform is the rugged Andes Mountain Range along Argentina's western border. The mountains are highest and widest in northern Argentina. The highest of these peaks is in Mendoza province at Cerro Aconcagua (22,841 feet above sea level). It is the highest mountain in the Western Hemisphere. Argentina's lake district—a popular tourist center—is in the southern Andes.

In northwestern Argentina, rivers that began hundreds of years ago in the mountains have carved deep valleys down the eastern side of the Andes. There are salt lakes in many of the basins between the mountains.

Nothing grows in the highest elevations of the Andes, which reach 13,000 feet. Nevertheless, the mountains are home to llamas, *guanacos* and *vicuñas* (both relatives of the camel), alpacas, and the Andean Condor (the largest flying land bird in the Western Hemisphere). The mighty Andean Condor is an endangered species.

In central west Argentina is a mountainous area called Cuyo, which is known for its viticulture (growing grapes).

Northern Plains and Andes Foothills

The northern plains to the east of the Andes are part of a large lowland area that extends north into Bolivia, Paraguay, and Brazil. This region is composed of two subregions: the Gran Chaco (called the Chaco) and Mesopotamia.

The Chaco extends east from the foothills to the Paraná River. It's a woodland area composed largely of grassy savanna with subtropical forests and plants. Several rivers cross the Chaco; they cause flooding during the summer. Since the soil isn't good for farming, much of the Chaco is used for grazing.

Mesopotamia lies between the Paraná and Uruguay rivers. This is a humid lowland of rolling prairies. It rises to forest in the northeast where rivers rush over the great Paraná Plateau. As a result, this area is known for its spectacular waterfalls—particularly the Iguaçu Falls on the border with Brazil.

In the warm and moist northeastern area of this region, you'll see many tropical plants such as the palm. The red *quebracho* provides extremely hard wood as well as tannin, an important ingredient in tanning leather. In the dry Andean regions of the northwest are many species of cacti.

In the north is Argentina's widest assortment of wildlife! Indigenous animals here include monkeys, jaguars, pumas, ocelots, anteaters, and tapirs. Birds include flamingos, parrots, and hummingbirds.

The Pampas
The humid Pampas (often called the Pampa) lie south of Chaco. These plains stretch west in a semicircle from Buenos Aires on the east coast for hundreds of miles.

Pampa

You won't see many trees in the Pampa, except for some imported species like the eucalyptus and sycamore planted along the roads. But you'll find plenty of native grasses! You'll also find rich, deep, black soil that makes this region one of the best farming areas on earth. Thus, much of Argentina's farming and industry are in the Pampa, along with much of the population.

The Pampa is also home to the legendary gauchos of the 18th century. These South American cowboys herded wild cattle and trained wild horses.

Patagonia
The lower part of Argentina that tapers to a point is composed of the rocky plateaus of Patagonia. They extend from low cliffs along the Atlantic coast to more than 5,000 feet at the base of the Andes in the west. The geography of this area includes canyons and valleys. The lowest point in the Western Hemisphere is Laguna del Carbón in Santa Cruz province at 344 feet below sea level.

Northern Patagonia ends in the lake district. Because of its rocky soil and fairly treeless land, people would have a hard time making a living in most of this area. So, few people live here.

Plant life in Patagonia consists of herbs, shrubs, and grasses. There are many fir, cypress, pine, and cedar trees in the Andes foothills. Wildlife here as well as in the Pampas includes armadillos, foxes, martens (a small animal related to the weasel), wildcats, hare, and deer. Birds include the American ostrich, hawks, falcons, herons, and partridges.

Major Rivers and Lakes
Most of Argentina's many rivers empty into the Atlantic Ocean. The Paraná (the largest) and Paraguay rivers join with the Uruguay near Buenos Aires. They form the Rio de la Plata River. This, in turn, forms part of the border between Argentina and Uruguay. The spectacular Iguaçu Falls is on the Iguaçu River, which is a tributary of the Paraná. Another important river is the Río Colorado, which forms the northern boundary of Patagonia.

The lake district in southern Argentina is a popular summer and winter tourist spot known for its many lakes, evergreen forests, and beautiful mountains and glaciers. The district extends from the Andes to Patagonia.

In northern Patagonia, the Nahuel Huapí Lake and the area surrounding it make up the Nahuel Huapí National Park. Lake Buenos Aires is shared with Chile.

A History of Argentina

Early Inhabitants

The earliest people to live in the Americas came from Siberia between about 60,000 and 8000 BCE. They probably walked to Alaska across a land bridge now covered by the Bering Strait. Then they spread to North and South America over thousands of years.

Those who came during this long migration period probably reached Argentina around 10,000 BCE. The Cave of the Hands in the Patagonia region is one of Argentina's oldest archaeological sites. It has beautiful and unusual cave paintings (mostly of hands) that date from around 7300 BCE.

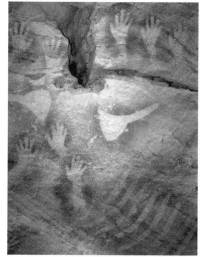

Cave of the Hands

By the time the Spanish arrived in the 1500s, much of today's Argentina was inhabited by nomadic tribes. They moved from place to place, hunting with weighted strips of leather called *boleadoras*. They could throw these weapons—which are still used today—great distances to catch an animal.

The native tribes in the northwest were very influenced by the highly advanced Incas. The Incan Empire expanded into Argentina from Peru in the 15th and 16th centuries. As a result, the northwest tribes were the most developed of Argentina's indigenous people. They practiced irrigated farming in the eastern foothills of the Andes.

The native people as far south as Tierra del Fuego were also hunter-gatherers. They wore little clothing but kept themselves warm with constant fires. They even lit fires in their canoes! The Spanish called this region *Tierra del Fuego,* which means *Land of Fire*.

Arrival of the Spanish

In the early 1500s, Spanish adventurers began exploring at the mouth of the Río de la Plata River that forms the border between Argentina and Uruguay. Not surprisingly, they were looking for treasures—especially silver. They were so sure of finding it that Spanish explorer Sebastian Cabot gave the great Rio de la Plata its name (River of Silver). He also called the new territory *Argentum* (which is Latin for *silver*). But he never found silver!

The Spaniard's first attempt to create a permanent settlement in 1536 at Buenos Aires on the Río de la Plata estuary failed after four years. They tried again and reestablished Buenos Aires in 1580. They continued to found settlements throughout the 16th century.

In 1599, members of the Jesuit Catholic religious order arrived in one of the new settlements—Córdoba. They founded what is now the National University of Córdoba, which is the fourth oldest university in the Americas. They also established about 30 missions in northeast Argentina. But the Spanish felt they were getting too powerful and expelled them from the country in 1767.

Independence

The British invaded Argentina twice between 1806 and 1807, when Spain was an ally of France in the Napoleonic Wars. But neither invasion was successful.

8

Toward the end of the 18th century, Argentine colonists who were prospering in the new land wanted to break free from the Spanish crown. After Napoleon invaded Spain in 1808, Buenos Aires declared its independence on May 25, 1810. Spain was eventually expelled from the entire continent by the 1820s.

San Martín

Under leaders such as General José de San Martín, the United Provinces of the Río de la Plata declared independence from Spain on July 9, 1816. These became the forerunners of the Argentine Republic. But some of the colonists resisted the power centered in Buenos Aires. There was bloody fighting for 20 years between those who wanted each province to govern itself and those who wanted the entire country's government in Buenos Aires.

In 1829, Juan Manuel de Rosas became governor of the Buenos Aires Province and focused the government's power there. His brutal 20-year term ended in 1852. He instituted the ruthless political police and tortured his enemies. He was finally forced from power by one of his former supporters—Justo José de Urquiza—who became the country's first president. Buenos Aires became the capital as well as South America's most important trade and cultural center.

The Argentine Golden Age

Argentina's third president, Domingo Faustino Sarmiento, was an educator and journalist. Under him, the young country advanced and grew. He is still honored and loved, especially for promoting education. During his time in office, a big wave of immigrants from Spain, Italy, Germany, and Eastern Europe crowded into Buenos Aires to work the port and other industries. Many of those who came from Italy and Spain between 1850 and 1930 helped influence the culture of Argentina today. From 1869 to 1895, the population of Buenos Aires grew more than 700 percent!

Argentina was booming—at least for people who were new to the country. But during this time, indigenous tribes lost their culture and way of life. Although the tribes in some regions like Patagonia and the southern Pampas fought fiercely against the colonists' control, the government wiped out much of the native population. This ruthless campaign, called Conquest of the Desert, doubled the area under state control. It also opened up Patagonia to settlement by the colonists and the sheep herding found there today.

Juan Perón

By the beginning of the 20th century, Argentina had a highly developed rail network that fanned out from Buenos Aires. But as immigration into the country grew, the economy began to decline. With the Great Depression of the 1930s, the military took over a country in which there was considerable unrest.

Colonel Juan Domingo Perón, one of Argentina's most loved—and hated—leaders, tried to deal with the country's economic crisis. He was President of Argentina three times, starting in 1946. His second wife, Eva (Evita) Duarte, was a popular radio actress who became a champion for the rights of women and the poor. She died at the age of 33 but remains popular (and controversial) to this day. *Evita,* a famous musical and a movie, is based on her life.

Perón knew the value of showmanship! He had lived in fascist Italy and Nazi Germany, where the dictators Mussolini and Hitler knew how to put on public shows of patriotism. He and Evita held massive public rallies and lived an extravagant life. Despite this, he improved wages and working conditions. He gave voting rights to working-class people and women. He gave everyone access to a university education. But he also censored the media and imprisoned or killed his political opponents.

Juan and Eva Perón

Evita's death in 1952 made him much less popular with the people. A violent military coup overthrew Perón's government, and he fled to Spain. He finally returned to Argentine political life in 1973 during a period of major economic and social problems. Perón was elected president once again, but he died in 1974. The country was in turmoil. His third wife and vice president, Isabel, took over as president.

Argentina in Chaos: The Dirty War

The anger that had been building in the Argentine people in the late 1960s and early 1970s boiled over into rioting against the government. Armed guerrilla groups rebelled against the military and the U.S. influence in Latin America. Isabel Perón created a death squad to destroy these revolutionary groups. This only caused more chaos.

A military coup in 1976 took control of the government in an effort to crush the armed guerillas and restore order. During a period called the Process of National Reorganization *(El Proceso)*, military security forces arrested, tortured, and killed suspected political opponents.

During the seven-year Dirty War *(Guerra Sucia)* that began in 1976, some 30,000 people were killed without standing trial. The Dirty War only ended in 1982 when the Argentine military tried to take control of the Falkland Islands from the British. The British had ruled the Falklands since 1833, but Argentina had claimed the islands as its own. The United Kingdom won the two-month Falklands War, and Argentina withdrew its forces. In the years that followed, few of the high-ranking officials responsible for the terrible human rights abuses in the Dirty War were ever convicted.

Into the Millennium

From 1990 well into the millennium, the country was on a roller coaster of government corruption. Many of the formerly state-run companies like the national oil company, the telephone company, and the postal service were sold off to foreign firms. Exports had slowed almost to a halt—especially farm products, which were a big part of the Argentine economy. By 2002 the Argentine economy had collapsed. People were emptying their bank accounts. They feared their money would disappear if they didn't actually have it in hand. Unemployment soared to more than 18 percent.

Once again, deadly rioting broke out over the government's failure to fix the economy. The country had five presidents in two weeks! All of them resigned rather than face the challenges. Finally, Eduardo Duhalde took office in January 2002. He announced that Argentina would not pay its $140 billion in foreign debt. Poverty skyrocketed, and foreign investors pulled out of the country.

Argentina Today

Duhalde's administration was able to stabilize the economy and pay off only the interest on its debt. But the climb back to a functioning government and a better economy continued to be difficult. Even though exports were once again booming by 2003, much of the country still lived in extreme poverty. About 25 percent of its people were unemployed.

In April 2003, Santa Cruz Governor Néstor Kirchner (called "K") won the presidential election. By the end of his term, he had become one of Argentina's most popular leaders. He cleaned up the government and tied up a lot of loose ends left from the Dirty War. He brought several high-ranking officers responsible for the killing during the Dirty War to trial for their crimes. He boosted the economy and paid off the country's debt. By the time he left office in 2007, unemployment had fallen to about nine percent.

Although poverty and inflation remain major issues, Argentina is moving forward once again. In 2007, Kirchner's wife, Senator Cristina Fernández de Kirchner, was elected its first female president by a landslide. She and her husband are often called "Bill and Hillary Clinton of the South." Her administration is continuing to work on Argentina's two major problems: poverty and inflation.

Today, Argentina is reaching out to the world once again. Its significant exports include grain, soybeans, sunflower seeds, grapes, peanuts, tea, clothing, leather goods, steel, electronics, and paper products. Tourists are flocking to the country's must-see destinations like Buenos Aires, the Andes, and Iguaçu Falls on the border with Brazil.

Daily Life

The Family Unit

Argentine family life used to be much more traditional than it is today. In prior decades, the father was the head of the family, and the mother was the head of the household. All generations of the family lived together in one house. Today, a typical Argentine family is much like any North American family. How a family lives is determined by where they live, how much money they make, and ethnic background.

Today many women work outside the home. Some families hire housekeepers to help with the chores. Young people often live with their parents until they get married. Men and women share the household responsibilities. Nowadays it's common to only have one or two kids.

The nuclear family is still highly valued and honored. Family members still gather each week for Sunday lunch and for special occasions like birthdays and holidays.

Argentine Architecture and Homes

The Cities
Much of the grander architecture in Argentina reflects the wealth and tastes of its Spanish and Italian landowners during colonial times. Larger cities like Buenos Aires have done a lot to preserve the buildings and city layout of their colonial past. Many public buildings and museums are likely to be former mansions of wealthy colonial land owners.

The larger cities were built in a specific layout, with a plaza in the center of the city surrounded by government buildings and a church. Plaza de Mayo, the main square in downtown Buenos Aires which was founded in 1580, is a perfect example of this. It is surrounded by several of the city's major landmarks, as well as *La Casa Rosada* (The Pink House), the seat of the executive branch of the government.

Also in the major cities you'll find large modern apartment buildings next to large business center skyscrapers in various architecture styles.

The Country
Particularly in southern Argentina, there are still many large rural country estates called *estancias*. Built in the 19th century by wealthy landowners, estancias were ranches for raising cattle, sheep, or horses. Many estancias are spectacular examples of colonial architecture with multiple buildings, a courtyard, and exquisite landscaping. Many of them have been converted into guest ranches.

Estancia

Going to School

Education is highly valued in Argentina, and the public schools are open to all. Children who are four or five can go to kindergarten, but this isn't required. School officially begins for kids at age six and ends at age 14. Public primary school is free, but there is no free transportation like a school bus. In rural areas, kids might go to school on horseback. On some large estancias, the children who live on the ranch have their own schoolhouse on the estate.

All students buy their own books. They also buy their own uniform—a white smock that looks like a lab coat. This is worn over regular clothes. Students who want to attend a private school sponsored by a church or other organization must pay tuition.

Students attend school in shifts. Some go from 8:00 AM to noon, and others go from 1:00 to 5:00 PM. Each session begins with raising the flag and singing the national anthem. There are three ten-minute breaks in each session.

Students who want to attend one of Argentina's public or private universities must go to secondary school for five years. Those who want careers in a trade such as agriculture can go to a vocational school.

Are We There Yet?

Bus

Argentina has excellent bus service in the major cities and between the cities and provincial areas. The main bus terminal in Buenos Aires, for example, has up to 2,000 arrivals and departures per day! There are many bus companies that serve many of the same destinations. Those traveling more than 100 miles will generally be able to get food, lots of leg room, and seats that recline into beds. It's like traveling in an airplane—on the ground.

Car

Some people drive cars in the cities, but it's easier to take the bus, walk, or ride a bike. Traffic regulations like speed limits are similar to those in the North America and Europe, but people often ignore them. Running red lights and rolling through stop signs are common.

The major highways in Argentina usually run only outside the large cities. Most of the country is connected by two-lane roads shared by buses, cars, and trucks. You can only get to some remote places on gravel or dirt roads.

Famous Argentinean: Che Guevara

Many people well-known for their work in entertainment, the arts, the sciences, religion, sports, public service, and politics come from Argentina. But no one has had such lasting international fame as Che Guevara.

Ernesto "Che" Guevara (1928–1967) is one of the world's most well-known revolutionaries. You have probably seen his image on posters, t-shirts, and hats. He is a folk hero more famous in death than he was in life.

Che Guevara

Che (pronounced SHAY) Guevara was a doctor, author, and guerrilla leader born in Rosario, Argentina. As a young medical student, he traveled throughout Latin America and was deeply disturbed by its great poverty. He concluded that the only way to help the poor was through a world revolution of social reform. He is most famous for joining Fidel Castro in overthrowing Cuban dictator Fulgencio Batista in 1959 and putting Castro in power. Che had several roles in the new Cuban government under Castro. He left the country in 1965 to start revolutions in the African Congo and in Bolivia. In 1967, he was captured and executed by Bolivian forces that were backed by the United States.

Even today, people debate whether Che Guevara was a hero or a villain. One thing is certain: he remains a symbol of social rebellion throughout the world.

Estancia Math

Beautiful horses are raised on large Argentine estancias. At various times in their lives, the horses are measured to see how much they have grown.

A horse's height is measured in inches by running a straight line from the ground to the highest point at the withers, which is just at the base of the neck. The total inches are then converted to *hands*. There are **four inches** in **one hand**. Therefore, if the horse below measures 60 inches, it is 15 hands high. 60 inches ÷ 4 inches (one hand) = 15 hands.

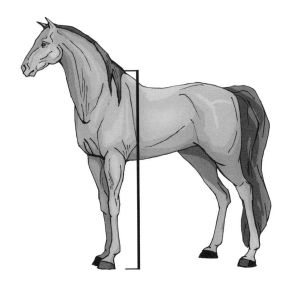

Use this formula to get the height, in hands, of the following horses.

1. If a horse is 72 inches, it is _____ hands high.

2. If a horse is 48 inches, it is _____ hands high.

3. If a horse is 52 inches, it is _____ hands high.

4. If a horse is 68 inches, it is _____ hands high.

5. If a horse is 64 inches, it is _____ hands high.

Did You Know?
The use of the term *hand* to measure a horse began long ago when people didn't have yard sticks or tape measures. So they simply used the width of their hands. Eventually, the term *hand* came to mean four inches. Every horse owner today still uses this term!

Language & Expressions

Language is the communication of thoughts and feelings through symbols, sounds, and gestures. The fun of learning about other countries is discovering how and why things are said, and what they mean. Every country has its unique way of communicating. Here are some fun facts about verbal and nonverbal communication in Argentina.

Famous Argentine Proverbs

A proverb is a saying that tells us something that is universally true about life. We commonly call them "words of wisdom." Here are four famous Argentine proverbs. What do you think they mean?

The one who loves you will make you weep.
A dog that barks all the time gets little attention.
If you have a tail of straw, then keep it away from the fire.
It's not the fault of the pig but of the one who scratches his back.

Body Language and Etiquette in Argentina

Body language is nonverbal communication. Etiquette is unwritten forms of behavior that people in a society are expected to follow. Here are some examples of body language and etiquette you'll find in Argentina.

When meeting a group of people, the introductions will be formal and follow a routine of introducing the eldest and most important person first.

When greeting people in informal situations, both women and men will kiss everyone present on the right cheek. Men may also slap each other on the back.

People physically stand closer together in conversation than people do in North America, and they may even touch each other while talking.

When leaving a party or other gathering, say goodbye to each person individually, if possible.

When invited to dinner, a guest is expected to bring a small gift for the host and/or hostess. But it's considered rude to bring knives or scissors—these indicate a cutting off of the relationship.

Gifts are always opened immediately.

Argentineans keep their hands visible while eating, but they do not rest their elbows on the table.

It is polite to leave a small amount of food on the plate, even when the meal is finished.

People indicate they have finished with a meal by resting their knife and fork across the plate with the prongs facing down and the handles facing to the right.

Know Before You Go

Although Argentineans speak Spanish, they refer to it as *castellano* rather than *español*. Even if you do speak Spanish, you are likely to hear many differences in the way Argentineans pronounce words compared to the way you learned to pronounce them.

Argentineans also use many *colloquialisms*—expressions used in casual conversation that are understood by speakers in that area. For example, you might hear one friend address another as "Che." Loosely translated, this means, "Hey, friend!" (The word comes from the famous revolutionary Che Guevara.)

Here are some common phrases you will use in Argentina. The spelling and pronunciation are also given. Try them out, then look up some additional ones!

English	Spanish	Pronunciation
Hello.	Hola.	OH-la.
What is your name?	¿Cómo se llama usted?	KOH-moh seh YA-mah oos-TEHD?
Good morning.	Buenas días.	booEHN-as DEE-as.
Good afternoon.	Buenas tardes.	booEHN-as TAR-dehs.
Good evening.	Buenas noches.	booEHN-as NO-chehs.
How are you?	¿Cómo está usted?	KOH-moh ehs-TA oos-TEHD?
I am fine.	Estoy bien.	ehs-TOY bee-EHN.
Please.	Por favor.	pohr fah-VOR.
Thank you.	Gracías.	gra-SEE-ahs.
You are welcome.	De nada.	deh NA-da.

1	uno	OO-no
2	dos	dos
3	tres	trace
4	cuatro	KWAT-ro
5	cinco	SINK-o
6	seis	saze
7	siete	see-YET-eh
8	ocho	OCH-o
9	nueve	new-EH-veh
10	diez	DEE-ace

FOODS

Daily Meals

Most people in Argentina eat four meals a day. Breakfast is a small, light meal with coffee or tea and milk, rolls or toast, butter, jam, or marmalade.

Lunch, which is served from 12:30 PM to 2:00 PM, usually includes meat and vegetables or salads. As in other European and Latin American countries, lunch used to be the main meal of the day. But this is changing since people who work can't afford to take time for a heavy meal at midday. Sunday lunch, however, remains the major meal of the week, with family members and extended family and friends getting together for several hours of eating and socializing.

In the late afternoon—perhaps after work—people go to cafés to drink coffee and eat *picadas* (small dishes of cheese, meats, seafood, olives, and peanuts). Or, they will simply take a break before dinner for tea or coffee with sandwiches or sweets like cookies, pastries, or cake. Although a light meal, this afternoon break is an important part of Argentine culture—especially in the cities where the cafés are packed all day! People love to get together at times like this over a snack to catch up on the latest soccer scores, talk politics, or just have a laugh with friends.

Dinner is served between 9:00 and 10:00 PM. This full meal will include a meat dish (usually beef).

Common Foods

People in all parts of Argentina tend to eat the same foods. Regional cuisine did not develop to the extent that it developed in other Latin American countries like Brazil. In fact, Argentineans still eat the dishes made with recipes brought over by their ancestors. And while fast food is very popular, people like to stick to the basics, like beef and pasta.

Beef
If you love beef, you'll love Argentina because beef is the national food. Argentine beef is generally considered the world's best. And it's no wonder! Argentine cattle graze freely on the fertile Pampas, which is some of the best grazing land in the world. *Asado* (barbecued meat) is an institution in Argentina, where anytime is a good time for a barbeque.

Italian Foods
The Italian immigrants brought their pastas, pizzas, and other flavorful foods. Italian cuisine has been one of Argentina's favorites since the great migration of Italians in the 18th century. Like steak houses, Italian restaurants and pizzerias are popular and found all over the country.

Pasta—particularly pasta bought fresh from the market—is a popular meal. Weekly Sunday lunch is likely to include a pasta dish. Sauces tend to be simple, like tomato with onion. Tubes or pillows of pasta are stuffed with cheese, but usually not with meat.

Pizzas in Argentina are nearly always made with thick crust. One popular pizza topping is *palmito,* a crunchy veggie that tastes like a cross between asparagus and celery. Argentine pizzas are big enough to be shared by several people.

Mate: The National Drink

Mate (MAH-te) is a South American drink made by steeping dried leaves of the yerba mate tree in hot water. Argentineans love this drink, and there are specific traditions associated with serving and drinking it. First, the yerba mate leaves are dried, chopped, and ground into a powder. Then a hollow gourd, which is also called a mate, is filled with the mixture. Hot, but not boiling, water is trickled into the gourd. The person preparing the drink follows a ritual for mixing the water and the powder in the gourd so that the mixture yields the best flavor.

Inserted into the gourd is the *bombilla*—a straw that was traditionally made of silver. (Today they're also made of stainless steel, aluminum, or tin.) The straw has small holes in the end inserted into the mate that block off the leaves in the hot water.

mate

Argentineans usually drink mate in social settings or for special occasions. Everyone sits in a circle and drinks the mate from the same gourd and straw. One person is the server who takes the first drink, which is generally considered the worst, and refills the gourd for each person.

Argentineans love this drink so much they'll carry a gourd along with hot water in a thermos wherever they go. They can replenish their hot water at shops, cafés, or gas stations with "Hot Water Available" signs in the window.

Some of the mate gourds are delicately carved or painted works of art. If you get to Argentina, consider buying a beautifully crafted mate as a souvenir.

Dulce de Leche and Other Sweets

Argentineans have a serious sweet tooth! *Dulce de leche*—one of its sweetest foods—is an Argentine invention. This thick caramel is made by boiling vanilla-flavored milk and sugar until it becomes so think you can eat it with a spoon—which is exactly how some people eat it. They also spread it on bread or biscuits, use it for cake filling, or put dollops of it on desserts. Some of the ice cream made in Argentina is flavored with dulce de leche. Although some people still make their own dulce de leche, most people today buy it at the store.

Other popular sweets are all kinds of cakes, cookies filled with jam or dulce de leche, pastries, *flan* (a creamy caramel served with custard or dulce de leche), and bread pudding. *Crepes* (thin pancakes served with sugar or rolled around a filling) are popular. *Gelato*—Italian ice cream—is a common treat that comes in a variety of flavors.

Snacks

Here are some favorite snacks *(minutas)* made at home or available from street vendors:

- *lomito*: a juicy slice of steak stuffed into pita bread
- *choripán*: an Argentine hot dog made with a hearty sausage
- *tostado*: a toasted cheese-and-ham sandwich
- *barrolucas*: an Argentine cheeseburger
- *empanadas*: pastry turnovers stuffed with beef, cheese, corn, ham, chicken, or other fillings

Holidays & Festivals

Revolution Day
May 25
This holiday commemorates the May Revolution of 1810, when Argentina appointed its own government in Buenos Aires after Napoleon invaded Spain. It's not a revolution in the traditional sense because there was no great military force or violence. But it is considered the first major step on the road to independence.

Traditionally this holiday was commemorated in Buenos Aires with a service at the Cathedral and a military parade. However, the celebration now rotates to different cities in the country, with Argentina's president attending the festivities.

National Flag Day
June 20
Flag Day commemorates the death of General Manuel Belgrano, who created the Argentine flag in 1812. Belgrano is one of Argentina's greatest heroes and was a leader in the country's fight for independence. Every year on June 20, national celebrations are held at the National Flag Memorial in the city of Rosario, northwest of Buenos Aires. And, of course, everyone displays the Argentine flag!

Independence Day
July 9
On this day in 1816, Argentina declared its independence from Spain. Argentina was not yet a country. The congressmen of the various provinces joined together in the northwest province of Tucumán to declare the United Provinces of South America independent.

July 9 is considered Argentina's birthday. People get together for parties with special foods. They proudly display the Argentine flag on their balconies or on the front of their home. People also honk their car horns—all day and all night!

Death of José de San Martín
August 17
The holiday remembers the death of General José de San Martín, who led Argentina's successful struggle for independence from Spain in the 19th century. San Martín is the national hero of Argentina. He is considered one of the key figures who helped liberate South America from Spain.

The Christmas Season and the New Year
December in Argentina is a hot month, so everyone is likely to be drinking cool beverages and sitting near the air conditioner rather than sitting by the fire. Nevertheless, the Christmas season is one of the most important and happiest of the entire year. Houses are decorated with garlands. Christmas trees are decorated with colored lights and ornaments. People may even put cotton on them to resemble snow! A nativity scene is placed near the tree. Wrapped gifts are tucked under the tree, and special foods are prepared throughout the season. One favorite is *panetone*, a sweet bread with nuts and crystallized fruit.

Christmas Eve, December 24
The main Christmas celebrations in Argentina take place on Christmas Eve. The extended family members go to church, then return home for an evening of dinner, music, and dancing. Candies are served just before midnight when the fireworks begin. After the fireworks, everyone opens gifts from *Papá Noel* (the Argentine Santa Claus).

Christmas Day, December 25

Christmas Day is taken up with religious services. Christmas dinner is likely to include a large meat dish like roast pork, turkey, or a steak dish—and, of course, lots of sweets! Some families may even have picnics or barbeques since the weather is hot. Families also get together to sing carols or go from house to house in the neighborhood.

New Year's Eve and New Year's Day, December 31 and January 1

Like many places in the world, New Year's Eve belongs to fireworks. People have a giant street party, singing and dancing until dawn. In Buenos Aires, there is a ticker tape parade. There will be more fireworks on New Year's Day.

The Feast of the Epiphany, January 6

This holiday honors the Three Wise Men who followed the star to Bethlehem, bringing gifts of gold, frankincense, and myrrh to the Christ child. On the evening of January 6th, children put their shoes beside the bed or under the Christmas tree to be filled with gifts and sweets by the Wise Men. The kids leave hay and water outside the house for the Wise Men's horses.

Carnival (Date Varies)

South American countries are famous for their spectacular annual Carnivals, and Argentina is no exception! Carnival is one of the biggest celebrations of the year. It begins two weeks prior to Lent, the solemn season of fasting before Easter.

Each region in Argentina celebrates Carnival in its own way. The town of Gualeguaychu, halfway between Buenos Aries and Iguaçu Falls, hosts the country's largest Carnival celebration. A Carnival center that seats thousands of people hosts samba clubs with more than 700 dancers, musicians, and singers competing for the "Kings of the Carnival" title. In Buenos Aires, every neighborhood is filled with street musicians (murgas) performing in parades. No matter where you land in Argentina at Carnival time, prepare for dancing, singing, costumes, and several days of one long street party!

Regional Festivals

People come from all over the world to celebrate the many regional festivals in Argentina. At the National Festival of Folklore each January in the central province of Córdoba, Argentina's best musicians, dancers, and actors pack the small town of Cosquín. Along with competitions in music and dance, you can see street theater and lots of arts and crafts displays. It's a good time to see some of the best tango dancers in the world.

July is a great time to visit Buenos Aires for the livestock show and fiesta celebrating the importance of the cattle industry.

A Snow Festival is held each August in the city of San Carlos de Bariloche in the southern Andes. (It's winter in August in Argentina.) Many of the area's residents are descended from settlers who came from Switzerland, so the festival includes Swiss foods.

Creative Arts

Music and Dance

The Tango

No music and dance are more closely associated with Argentina than the tango, which became popular in Latin America in the early 20th century. In Argentina, the tango originated in lower-class neighborhoods of Buenos Aires, but it didn't take long to spread to the rest of the world.

The tango is a graceful dance in which two people essentially walk to the music. The dancers take a variety of long steps and hold a series of long poses. When the tango first became popular in the early 1900s, some people thought it was disgraceful. But the tango still caught on, and different regions developed their own tango styles. To-day the tango is as popular as ever—both the dance and the music that accompanies it. The instruments traditionally used in tango music are the *bandoneón* (a type of accordion), the violin, and the guitar.

Tango dancers

Buenos Aires hosts an annual Tango Festival between February and March. The tango is such an important cultural element that it was declared a world heritage of humanity in 2009 by UNESCO (the United Nations Educational, Scientific, and Cultural Organization).

The Zamba

Another popular dance is the *zamba*, which is the national folk dance of Argentina. It is a stately, slow dance in which couples circle each other, waving white handkerchiefs. Zambas have been composed on many subjects, including Argentine history, the beauty of the land, or political protest. Zamba music is played primarily on the guitar and *bombo legüero*, a large drum traditionally made from a hollow tree trunk.

The Gaucho

Few figures play a more important part in the national identity of Argentina than the *gaucho*. The gaucho is the equivalent of the American cowboy and is celebrated in song, dance, poetry, and folklore.

The gaucho culture began in the 16th century when cattle and horses escaped from the early Spanish settlements to become free-roaming herds. But the 100-year period from about 1750 to 1850 is the era of the gaucho. During that time, and still today, Argentina's greatest source of wealth were the huge herds of cattle and wild horses that roamed the Pampas. The men who left the cities for the Pampas in order to tame horses and track down lost cattle for ranchers became known as *gauchos*. These rugged horsemen lived an isolated life. They wrote poems and songs about their adventures.

Gaucho

The distinct gaucho outfit included a poncho, loose-fitting trousers that could be tucked into boots, and a belt. The poncho doubled as a saddle blanket. Their weapons included only a knife, a whip, a rope, and the weighted strips of leather called *boleadoras* that they could throw great distances to ensnare an animal. Both gaucho pants and the poncho have been adapted into popular women's fashions.

The grand era of the gaucho ended when the Pampas were fenced off into huge estates. Gauchos sought work on the cattle ranches, which is where you will find them today.

The legendary gaucho is celebrated in Argentine literature, music, and art as a strong, brave, honorable wanderer. They are honored at a festival in the Pampas every December.

Spelling Match

Circle the word in each row that matches the word on the left. Do this as quickly as you can!

1. Argentina	Aryentina	Argentena	Argentina	Arentina
2. Buenos Aires	Benos Aires	Buenos Aires	Buenos Airs	Buenos Air
3. Pampas	Pampas	Pamppas	Pampass	Pamas
4. Andes	Andys	Andes	Ands	Ants
5. Patagonia	Padagonia	Patagoni	Patagona	Patagonia
6. Iguaçu	Iguaça	Iguaçi	Iguaçu	Iguaçua
7. Juan Perón	Juan Persón	Juan Peróne	Jan Perón	Juan Perón
8. Tierra del Fuego	Tiara del Fuego	Tiera del Fuego	Tierra del Fueg	Tierra del Fuego
9. Falklands	Falkland	Falklands	Falklends	Falklend
10. Plaza de Mayo	Plaza di Mayo	Plaza del Mayo	Plaza de Maya	Plaza de Mayo
11. La Casa Rosada	La Casa Rosada	Le Casa Rosada	La Casa Rosado	La Casa Rosad
12. Che Guevara	Che Guevara	Che Gwevara	Che Guevera	Che Guevere
13. Spanish	Spanlish	Spanesh	Spanish	Spanishe
14. Italian	Italiane	Italian	Italy	Itallian
15. Manuel Belgrano	Manual Belgrano	Manuel Belgran	Manuel Belgrano	Manuel Belgrono
16. José de San Martin	José de San Martin	José de Sant Martin	Joséy de San Martin	José de San Martine
17. Cosquín	Cosquín	Cousin	Cuisine	Cosquínt
18. Chile	Chily	Chilly	Chile	Child
19. Uruguay	Uraguay	Urugway	Uruguaye	Uruguay
20. Inti	Inte	Inti	Inni	Into

Sports & Games

Football

Argentina is a world-class star in football (some other countries refer to it as *soccer*). It holds the world record for the most international titles won by any international team. Football is part of the country's culture. Everyone plays it: men and women, kids and adults. They play it indoors and outdoors, all over the country.

Argentina is currently the sixth most successful team in the world and has won all sorts of major tournaments. It has won the FIFA (International Federation of Association Football) World Cup twice and the Copa América (the main South American men's football competition) 14 times. Its greatest football rival is Brazil.

Football

Argentine Horses

Argentineans' love of horses dates back to the early Spanish conquerors, who brought horses with them when they settled the land. Thanks to the great plains of the Pampas, horses multiplied in Argentina. Today you will find the finest horses in the world here, including thoroughbreds and native Argentine horses called *criollos*. Every kind of horse sport is found in Argentina. Horse riders from all over the world come to Argentina to pick out their next prize-winning mount.

Polo

In polo, two teams of players on horseback try to drive a small ball through each other's goal with a mallet. Argentina is *the* polo-playing nation of the world. For more than 60 years, it has been the world's polo champion.

Argentina raises some of the best polo pony stock in the world and produces most of the world's top players. The Argentine Open, the Hurlingham Open, and the Tortugas Open—three of the most important international polo tournaments—are all held in Argentina.

Polo

Pato

Juan Perón declared *pato* the official game of Argentina in 1953. It is a combination of polo and basketball played on horseback.

Two teams of four members each fight to get a six-handled ball. They score by throwing a ball through a vertical ring. (This differs from basketball where the ball is thrown through a *horizontal* ring). The rings are about three feet around and located on poles that are about eight feet high. The winning team is the one that scores the most goals after six eight-minute periods.

Pato is Spanish for *duck*. When the game was played in prior centuries, a live duck was used instead of a ball! The playing field would stretch between cattle ranches. The first team to reach its own ranch house with the duck was the winner.

Argentina at the Olympics

Argentina first participated in the Olympic Games in 1900. Since that time, it has won 66 medals in the Summer Olympic Games. Seven of those medals were in boxing, two were in football, and two were in polo.

Sports for Everybody

For those who want to play on the weekends, the varying terrain of Argentina offers lots of sports options. You can hike or rock climb in the Andes. You can horseback ride, especially in the central and northern regions. You can go rafting, hot air ballooning, or paragliding. You can cycle anywhere. Near the tip of the continent, you can dog sled in Tierra del Fuego!

Card Games

Card games are extremely popular in Argentina with kids and adults. One of the most popular games is *truco* (trick). This game supposedly originated with country gentlemen who used subtle movements to warn their partners of the other players' strategies. Bluffing and signaling your partner about the cards you hold are big parts of this game. The signals vary from region to region, or partners can develop their own signals. For example, raising the eyebrows, closing both eyes, and closing one eye only are all signals for types of cards in a hand.

Hello from Argentina!

Imagine you are a vacationing tourist in one of these areas of Argentina:

- the Pampas
- the Andes
- Patagonia
- Tierra del Fuego
- Buenos Aires

Write a post card to a friend or relative and tell the person a few things you have done or seen in this region. Use the Internet or other resources to find out about the area you've chosen. Consider what you have learned as a tourist about the people, the land, or anything else you consider interesting!

Dear _____:

Brazil

GUYANA
Georgetown

SURINAME
Paramaribo

FRENCH GUIANA
Cayenne

Guiana Highlands

MARAJÓ IS.

Rio Negro

Amazon R.

Manaus⊠

Belém

PERNAMBUCO

Fortaleza

The Selvas

PARÁ

Madeira R.

CEARÁ

BRAZIL

Recife

AMAZONAS

Sierra do Roncador

Brazilian Highlands

São Francisco R.

BAHIA

Salvador

Plateau of
Mato Grosso

Brasília

MINAS GERAIS
Belo
Horizonte

Paraná R.

SÃO PAULO

RIO DE JANEIRO

Rio de Janeiro

PARANÁ

São Paulo

Curitiba

Atlantic Ocean

RIO GRANDE
do SUL

Pôrto Alegre

N

10°
5°
0°
5°
10°
15°
20°
25°
30°
35°

70°   65°   60°   55°   50°   45°   40°   35°

0   100   300   500 mi.

0 100 300   500 km

Welcome to Brazil!

The mixed cultural heritage of Brazil is unlike that of any other country on earth. Regardless of their ethnic origin, all Brazilians share the belief that they are one people with a common history and common goals. Combine this national unity with spectacular scenery and ecosystems teeming with life, and you have a glittering global gem. As if all this wasn't enough, Rio de Janeiro will host the Summer Olympic Games in 2016—the first to be held in Brazil.

After you have finished learning about Brazil, be sure to check out page 148 for additional classroom activities.

FAST FACTS

Official Name: Federative Republic of Brazil

Location: Eastern South America, bordering the Atlantic Ocean

Population: 198,739,269 (2010 estimate)
About half the population is under age 30.

Capital City: Brasília

Area: 3,287,597 square miles. Brazil is the largest country in South America. It shares common boundaries with every South American country except Chile and Ecuador. It is slightly smaller than the mainland United States.

Major Language: Portuguese

Major Religion: Roman Catholic: 73.6%
Protestant: 15.4%
Afro-Brazilian religions

Currency: The real (R$)   1 real = 100 centavos

Climate: Mostly tropical, but temperate in the south

The Land: Mostly flat to rolling lowlands in the north; some plains, hills, mountains, and a narrow coastal belt

Type of Government: Federal republic

Flag and Motto:

The Brazilian flag is green with a large yellow diamond in the center. On the diamond is a blue globe with 27 white five-pointed stars (one for each state in the country along with the Federal District). These are arranged in the same pattern as the night sky over Brazil. The blue globe has a white equatorial band with the motto ORDEM E PROGRESSO (Order and Progress).

Coat of Arms:

The coat of arms consists of the central emblem surrounded on the left by coffee branches and on the right by tobacco branches. (These were important crops when the coat of arms was created in 1889, just after Brazil became a republic.) In the blue circle in the center is the Southern Cross (also called the Crux). This is the smallest of the 88 constellations, but it can easily be seen in the Southern Hemisphere. The ring of 27 stars around it represents the 26 states of Brazil and the Federal District. The blue ribbon contains the official name of Brazil: República Federativa do Brasil (Federative Republic of Brazil) in its first line. In the second line is the date of the Federative Republic's establishment: November 15, 1889.

National Flower: Ipê-amarelo

National Animals: Jaguar
Sabiá (Thrush, a songbird)

Natural Environment

Brazil is the largest country in Latin America. It occupies half of the South American continent and a third of the region of Latin America. Most of Brazil's territory is in the tropical zone, between the equator and the Tropic of Capricorn.

Because of its tremendous territory and position on the globe, Brazil has a great variety of landforms, climate and vegetation zones. It's rightfully called the "Land of Contrasts."

Brazil also has an immense river system. The Amazon River in the north is the world's largest river system. In the south, the Paraná-Paraguay-Uruguay is the world's seventh largest river system. The São Francisco is Brazil's third largest river.

Five Geographical Regions
Brazil has five distinct geographical regions: Amazonia, the Northeast Region, the Southeast Region, the Southern Region, and the Central-West Region.

Amazonia
Amazonia, the North Region, is the largest region but the smallest in population. It lies primarily in the lowlands and within the Amazon River basin near the equator that divides the Northern and Southern Hemispheres. Its climate is hot and dry. Amazonia has the world's largest and densest tropical rainforest. It spans more than half of Brazil. (Sixty percent of the entire rainforest lies within Brazil.)

The economy of Amazonia is based on mining, forest products, agriculture, and fishing. Most of the population is centered in the city of Manaus in the interior of the Amazon River basin. People are also scattered along the river in small towns and settlements. Belém, the port city at the mouth of the Amazon River, gets up to 100 inches of rain in the winter. It's no surprise that the main form of transportation here is the boat!

Northeast Region
The Northeast Region is a land of sharp contrasts with rich soil and heavy rainfall along the coast and dry lands prone to drought in the interior. The Northeast's seacoast was the area first colonized by the Portuguese. This area was also strongly influenced by the African slaves brought to seacoast towns like Recife and Salvador.

The Northeast Region's economy is diverse. Tropical crops such as sugar cane, rice, and cacao are grown along the seacoast; there is a lot of oil exploration offshore. People raise cattle in the interior. Cotton, beans, corn, and *sisal* (a plant that produces a stiff fiber) are grown here, too.

Southeast Region

This is truly the economic, social, and political heart of Brazil. Seventy percent of Brazil's population lives here on less than one-third of the area of the entire country. Most of Brazil's industries, roads, and railroads are here, along with its three largest cities of São Paulo, Rio de Janeiro, and Belo Horizonte.

The coast of the Southeast Region is tropical; the upland interior is dry and temperate. The entire region is rich in minerals like iron ore, gold, platinum, silver, and gemstones like diamonds. With the discovery of gold, diamonds, and other precious minerals, the interior state of Minas Gerais has become one of the world's richest mining areas.

Southern Region

This region differs greatly from the rest of the country. It is the smallest. With its semi-tropical climate, it occasionally gets frost and snow. Many of the *gaúchos* (Brazil's cowboys) in this region live on farms and plantations where they raise cattle, horses, and hogs. The larger cities have a variety of industries.

Central-West Region

This huge region is second only to Amazonia in size. The government wanted to encourage people to move away from the heavily populated seacoasts and move toward the country's under-populated interior. So Brazil's capital was moved to a planned, modern city in the Central-West Region called Brasília. Not surprisingly, the Central-West area is also called the "Pioneer Region."

Plants and Animals

Brazil's vast territory is a treasure trove of biological diversity! The Amazon Rainforest, for example, has the greatest biological diversity in the world. Scientists estimate that there are some 4 million plant and animal species in Brazil. But this is just an estimate—new species are found all the time.

Larger mammals include large cats such as pumas, jaguars, and ocelots. Unusual ones you may not have heard of are *peccaries* (they resemble pigs) and *tapirs* (they're pig-like, too). More familiar are foxes, anteaters, sloths, opossums, and armadillos. The rare bush dog is found in the rainforest, as are monkeys of many species. Deer abound in the south.

The Amazon Rainforest

The Amazon Rainforest is the largest tropical rainforest in the world. It is an environmental treasure *and* an international concern.

The Amazon River, which flows east from the Andes Mountains in Peru to the Atlantic Ocean, is about 4,195 miles long. It is the longest river in the world and carries the most water. The Amazon basin encompasses about 1.7 billion acres; about 1.4 billion acres of this land is covered by the rainforest. This region includes territory of nine nations; most of the rainforest is in Brazil.

The Amazon Rainforest is incredibly important to our planet. It is home to many people and has the largest collection of plant and animal species in the world. This includes about 40,000 species of plants, 3,000 fish, 1,294 birds, 427 mammals, 428 amphibians, and 378 reptiles. The rainforest helps stabilize our global climate. It recycles and cleans water. It removes carbon dioxide from the atmosphere and stores it in the roots, stems, leaves, and branches of its plants and trees, which it then changes into oxygen and sends back out into the world. Its plants are also a vital source of medicine.

But the rainforest is in serious danger. Due to human settlement, land development, clearing land for cattle pastures, and logging, many acres are being destroyed. As a result, the heavy rains on the cleared land are washing away the top soil layer and upsetting the balance of the rich ecosystem. (An *ecosystem* is a group of things that live together and need each other to exist. In the rainforest, for example, humans, trees, plants, birds, bugs, reptiles, mammals, amphibians, and soil are all vitally linked.)

With the rainforest gone, the rare and wonderful plants and animals that live there will cease to exist. Our atmosphere would not be well regulated. We would not have the many useful products that come from it, like fine woods, the cacao bean that is made into chocolate, sugar cane, bananas, and medicines.

People all over the world are seriously worried about the loss of the Amazon Rainforest. Scientists, governments, businesses, and citizens are all searching for ways to harvest its treasures without destroying it in the process.

Amazon Rainforest

Layers of the Rainforest

Like every other forest, the rainforest has layers. Each layer is a mini-system. Some creatures live in several layers. Others live in just one. Each layer is vital to the whole system.

Forest Floor: Damp, infertile, and thin. Many creatures like snakes, ocelots, worms, and bugs live in and use this layer to hunt for food.

Shrub: Begins about 4 feet above the ground. Dim. Looks as it if is filled with houseplants that have gone wild.

Understory: Stretches between the canopy and the shrub layers. Populated with monkeys, ants, and snakes.

Canopy: 70 to 90 feet high. Composed of intertwined branches and vines. Filled with birds, monkeys, snakes, sloths, and other creatures that live in trees at least part of the time.

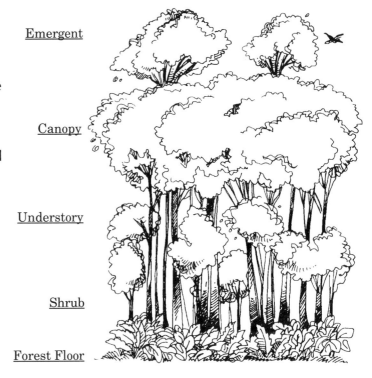

Emergent: The tallest layer that gets more sun than the other layers. Made up of a few tall, wide trees that can reach 250 feet high. Home to a variety of butterflies and birds.

Creatures of the Amazon

Below are 12 boxes with a picture of an Amazonian fish, bird, mammal, amphibian, reptile, or insect in each one. Using this list, write the correct name of each in the box. Try to guess the ones you may not have heard of, or look them up using books or the Internet.

alligator	macaw	poison arrow frog
armadillo	manatee	rhinoceros beetle
capybara	mosquito	sloth
jaguar	piranha	spider monkey

1. _____

2. _____

3. _____

4. _____

5. _____

6. _____

7. _____

8. _____

9. _____

10. _____

11. _____

12. _____

A History of Brazil

Early Inhabitants

Archaeologists think the earliest inhabitants of the Americas came from Siberia between about 60,000 and 8000 BCE. They probably simply walked from Siberia to Alaska across a land bridge now covered by the Bering Strait. Then they spread to North and South America over thousands of years.

The people who came to the Americas during this long period of migration were probably in Brazil about 50,000 years prior to the arrival of the Portuguese in 1500 CE. By that time, there were 2 million to 4 million natives living in more than 1,000 tribes. But these early people did not develop a highly advanced civilization like the Incas who established an empire from northern Ecuador to central Chile. Apart from some rock paintings and a few bits and pieces of human life found in the Amazon region, we know little about Brazil's earliest people.

Arrival of the Portuguese

Brazil's history as we know it began in the 16th century, when Spain and Portugal had conflicting claims on territory throughout the world. This disagreement was resolved by drawing an imaginary north-south line on the map that gave all lands west of the line to Spain and all lands east of the line to Portugal. According to this agreement, the territory of what is now Brazil belonged to Portugal.

In 1500, Pedro Álvares Cabral reached the Brazilian coast with a fleet of more than ten ships. The fleet was bound for East Africa and Asia to set up trading posts. No one knows whether the ships were blown off-course or whether they intended to visit South America. They christened the land *Terra da Vera Cruz* (Land of the True Cross) and left to explore what they thought were richer lands.

It wasn't until 1531 that a Portuguese fleet arrived with about 400 men ready to make this new land their home—at least temporarily. They established the first settlement at São Vicente near the current port of Santos. The settlers' lives were extremely hard due to the hostile Indians and competition from Dutch and French settlers.

In 1549, Portugal's king sent Tomé de Sousa to be the first governor of Brazil. The 1,000 settlers that came with him were Portuguese officials, soldiers, prisoners, Christians, and the first six Jesuit priests. The city of Salvador, where they settled, became Brazil's capital until 1763, when it was moved to Rio de Janeiro.

The Indigenous People's Struggle

At the arrival of the Portuguese, Brazil's indigenous people were farmers along the Amazon or nomadic tribes of hunter-gatherers. The Guarani, the Tupi, and the Tapuia were the three key groups along the coast. The Guarani and Tupi had similar language and culture. (Some in Amazonia still speak an adapted form of the Tupi-Guarani language.) The Tupi became best known to the Europeans, who adopted many Tupi names for Brazil's animals, rivers, mountains, and towns that are still used today.

Over the following centuries, Brazil's Indians virtually lost their way of life. Early Portuguese settlers enslaved the Tupi and other Indian tribes to work in the sugarcane fields. Many were worked to death. Others died of diseases brought by the settlers. About 500,000 were killed or enslaved by the 17th and 18th century *bandeirantes*—adventurers from São Paolo who set out for Brazil's interior, looking for treasures. Finally, Jesuit missionaries outlawed Indian traditions and customs, moved them to missions, and forced them to adopt the Christian religion and lifestyle.

Today, Brazil's indigenous population is only between 350,000 and 600,000 at best. Most of them live in the isolated Amazonian forests. They have had a very hard time maintaining their cultural identity.

Africans and Slavery

By the 1550s, wealthy Brazilian sugar plantation owners began buying African slaves to work the plantations. The slaves were torn from their families and transported to Brazil by ship in horrible, inhuman conditions. Once on the plantations, they were forced to convert to Catholicism. They were treated poorly and forced to toil up to 17 hours daily in searing heat.

Many died of disease and starvation. Others starved themselves to death rather than continue. Some simply refused to work, and some even fled and formed communities of ex-slaves in the countryside. There are more than 700 villages in Brazil today that started as these refugee slave communities. Some were so isolated from modern society that they have only come in contact with white Brazilians in the last 20 to 30 years.

By the time slavery was abolished in Brazil in 1888, about 3.6 million Africans had been shipped to the country. Even after slavery became illegal, African slaves were still smuggled into Brazil.

Many Portuguese settlers married the indigenous Indians and African slaves. You can still see this cultural mix in Brazilians today. Brazil has more people with black ancestors than any other nation on the globe apart from Africa.

The Gold Boom

The bandeirantes who were responsible for killing so many of Brazil's Indians discovered gold in the current state of Minas Gerais in southeastern Brazil. For part of the 18th century, Brazil was the world's greatest producer of gold. Boom towns sprang up. Rich merchants built beautiful mansions and put up the money for baroque-style churches, many of which remain today. By the end of the 18th century, the population in this area was half a million. About one-third of the 2 million slaves brought to Brazil in the 18th century worked the gold fields—which often proved to be far worse for them than working in the sugarcane fields. The gold boom declined by about 1750.

Independence

Brazil was under Portuguese rule for more than three centuries. But in 1789, a movement for independence grew out of people's resistance to paying taxes to Portugal. The movement was headed by Joaquim José da Silva Xavier, a dentist called *Tiradentes* (Tooth Puller), along with eleven other conspirators. But their plans failed. The conspirators were exiled to other countries, and Tiradentes was hanged in Rio de Janeiro in 1792. Nevertheless, he became a national martyr and a symbol of resistance to the Portuguese monarchy.

Brazil became an independent nation just 30 years later, in 1822. A military coup, supported by Brazil's coffee farmers, declared Brazil a republic in 1889. (By this time, coffee had become the main export.) The military and Brazil's land-owning coffee growers became the dominant political force until Getúlio Vargas came to power in 1930.

Immigration

In the 1890s, millions of immigrants from Italy, Japan, Spain, Germany, Portugal, and elsewhere flocked to Brazil to work the coffee plantations. The ethnic mixture in Brazil today is partially due to this immigration—especially in cities like Rio de Janeiro and São Paulo, where they settled. Most Brazilians today have some combination of European, African, Asian, and Middle Eastern ancestry.

Brazil Today

The military remained in power until 1985, when the regime ended peacefully and civilian rulers took over the government. Democracy was reestablished with the enactment of the current Federal Constitution in 1988. Free elections were held that year and continue to be held to this day.

Over the past 50 years, Brazil has survived military coups, an unstable economy, and political repression. But it has emerged from all of this stronger than ever! It is the largest and most densely populated South American country with the sixth largest population in the world. It is one of the most multicultural nations on earth. It is increasingly becoming a global force.

Its once unstable economy is now South America's leading economy. Foreign investors are pouring money into the country. Its industry and agriculture continue to develop. Brazil's booming export business is sending products such as aircraft, coffee, automobiles, soybeans, orange juice, steel, ethanol, textiles, footwear, and electrical equipment all over the world. Of course, no discussion of Brazil's best exports is complete without mentioning gemstones! Brazil is one of the gem capitals of the world. Buyers from all over treasure its diamonds, tourmaline, amethysts, quartz, and topaz.

Although the poverty rate remains high, social programs are helping to feed, house, and educate the poor. In 2007, the government launched a four-year plan to spend $300 billion to upgrade the country's roads, power plants, and ports. In 2016, Brazil will open its doors to the world when Rio de Janeiro hosts the Summer Olympic Games.

Take a Trip to Iguaçu Falls

Iguaçu Falls is one of Brazil's national treasures and one of the great natural wonders of the world. Proofread the passage below. Circle the 15 spelling and grammar errors. Write the correct word above the incorrect one.

Iguaçu Falls

Iguaçu Falls, which lies on the Brazil/Argentine border, is one of the worlds most spectacular sites. Iguaçu means *big water* in the Tupi Indian langwage. The 296 cascades in the shape of a horseshoo that make up the falls span more than two miles across. Once youve seen Iguaçu Falls, you will never forget the tons of water rushing of the cliffs and the mists rising from the jungel below.

One of the best ways to experience the Iguaçu Falls from the Brazilan side is to take a boat trip to get next to and sometimes under the faling water. You first board a truck that takes you through the jungle to the dock where you then board a boat. You put on your raincoat and life preserver and tuck your valubles into a plastic bag. Imaging your excitemen as you navigate through the rapids, listening to the crashing water mixed with the roaring of the boat motors. The sound is so loud, you can't hear yourself talk!

The captain knows the rapids well. He or she dips the boat into the water a few times just to soak the pasengers! The river is rocky, so you won't cruise too close to the big falls. But you'll be able to cruise under some of the smaller ones. And you wont even notice that your thoroghly soaked—despite your raincoat. But who cares about getting wet when you're experiencing one of the most breathtaking places on the plant?

Daily Life

About two-thirds of all Brazilians live on or near the coast. Many rural people have gone to the cities to live and look for work.

There are striking contrasts between the rich and the poor in Brazil. The richest ten percent of Brazilians make about half of the income in the country. The poorest ten percent make less than one percent of the country's income.

Many aspects of a person's life are determined by the economic class into which he or she is born. This will include what school a person attends (if he or she attends school at all), the neighborhood where one lives, where one shops, the sports one gets to play, the foods one eats, and the kind of housing where one lives. Despite the incredible wealth, many people in Brazil remain trapped in poverty.

The Family Unit

The family is the building block of Brazilian culture and the single most important institution in the country. Powerful families have dominated the economic, political, and religious life of Brazil for centuries.

"Family" encompasses more than the nuclear family of mother, father, and children. It also includes a larger, extended *parentela* (kinship group) of grandparents, aunts and uncles, and their families. Older family members are highly respected for their experience and wisdom. They are very influential in shaping the values of the kids in the family group.

Brazilian family members like to live close to each other. Grown children usually remain at home until they are married. Even after marriage, they will likely live near their parents and have a lot of weekly contact. Members of an extended family may even live in the same apartment building.

Brazilian Houses

The housing in Brazil consists of apartment buildings and single-family homes. Many Brazilian buildings are decorated with brightly colored tile mosaics on the outside walls. Sometimes sidewalks are made of mosaics in patterns like ocean waves.

In the countryside, the wealthiest farm families live on *fazendas,* or plantations. Middle-class families live in houses made of stone with stucco walls and clay tile roofs. The poorest families live in small houses made of woven branches and plastered with mud.

In the cities, those who cannot afford to live in apartments and single-family homes must live in the *favelas*—very crowded and run-down neighborhoods—that are found in all major cities. Their homes look like temporary shelters built of cardboard, bits of wood and metal, and other scraps. Often there is no running water. Sadly, many children of the favelas spend most of their time in the streets. They are part of Brazil's large population of the extremely poor who live well below the poverty line.

To Market, To Market!

Although Brazil has modern supermarkets and shops, only those in the middle and upper classes can afford to shop in them. But people of all economic levels shop in the public markets. The *dia de feira,* or market day, is an old tradition. Even the Portuguese names for Monday through Friday are market terms. Monday is *segunda-feira* (second market), Tuesday is *terça-feira* (third market), and so on through Friday. Only Saturday and Sunday have names that indicate the day.

Each stall of the feira specializes in a certain product, such as vegetables, eggs, flowers, fruit, cereals, and leather goods.

Are We There Yet?

Brazil has the largest network of roads in Latin America. Those who can afford cars own them for in-city driving and weekend exploring. But driving in Brazil can be dangerous! There are definitely rules and regulations, but people often don't follow them. Drivers tailgate, run red lights, or ignore stop signs when there is no oncoming traffic. They're not keen on slowing down for pedestrians in crosswalks. In rural areas, you have to watch out for animals wandering onto the roadway.

For those who don't have a car and can't walk to school or work, the bus is a common way to get around. It's also a great way to travel to other cities. Most cities of more than 100,000 people will have a bus line to the larger cities close by. There is no one bus company that serves all of Brazil.

Most cities have extensive bus services. But often the bus stops are unmarked; locals just know the information. The buses themselves will display a sign on the windshield that tells their main destinations. People just wave for the bus to stop. Buses from many different lines may be picking up passengers at the same stops—which can get confusing! Some people stand in the middle of the street to make sure their bus stops for them.

Riding a bicycle is still the way most people get around in the rural areas. People don't use bicycles much in the big cities, except for Rio de Janeiro and Recife where there are bicycle tracks along the beaches.

If you make it to the Amazon region, prepare for a boat ride, since that's just about the only way to get around there. Amazon River boats connect northern Brazil with Peru, Venezuela, and Colombia, but it's a long, hot journey to any of these countries by boat!

Going to School

Brazilian kids under age six can go to school, but this is only an option. There are nurseries for children under two, kindergartens for kids two to three years old, and preschools for kids four to six years old.

Children ages six to 14 must go to school for fundamental education. Year 1 is a preschool to get kids off to a good start in reading and writing. The government sets the curriculum that kids must study. Throughout years 2, 3, 4, and 5, kids study Portuguese, history, geography, science, math, arts, and physical education. Kids in years 6, 7, 8, and 9 add one or two foreign languages (usually English and Spanish). Each region supplements this core curriculum as it sees fit for the students in that area.

During years 1 through 5 of fundamental education, each group of students has one teacher. For years 6 through 9, each group will have many teachers. In addition to their studies, students in all years of fundamental education will have at least 800 hours of additional activities per year. The schools will set their own calendars and times for student participation. In the country, students' schedules will be worked around the planting and harvesting seasons.

Secondary education is three years long. Students will study Portuguese (including Portuguese language and literature), a foreign language (usually English or Spanish), history, geography, math, physics, chemistry, biology, philosophy, and sociology. During the second and third year of secondary education, students can take vocational training to study for a profession in the trades.

Getting into university is very difficult. Candidates for entrance take public open exams that last about one week and take place only once a year. Public universities in Brazil are free, so the competition to get in is difficult. Brazilian public universities are highly regarded and focus as much on conducting research as they do on education.

Famous Brazilian: Pelé

Edison Arantes do Nascimento (1940—), better known to the world as Pelé, is Brazil's most famous sports star and one of the best-known people ever born in the country. This well-known football (soccer) player is a global sporting legend and a national hero in Brazil. The International Olympic Committee gave him the title of Athlete of the Century. In 1999, *Time* magazine designated him one of the 100 Most Important People of the 20th Century. He is the highest-leading scorer of the Brazil National Football Team and the only player in the world to have three World Cup medals. Retired since 1977, he supports improving the social conditions of the poor in Brazil, especially the children.

Pelé

Language & Expressions

Here are some fun facts about verbal and nonverbal communication in Brazil.

Famous Brazilian Proverbs

Here are eight famous Brazilian proverbs. What do you think they mean?

He who knows nothing doubts nothing.
The tree with most leaves will not necessarily produce juicy fruit.
You can only take out of a bag what is already in it.
One man's happiness is another man's sadness.
Half a loaf is better than none.
Grain by grain, the hen's stomach is full.
Only the wearer knows where the shoe pinches.
Between the beginning and the end there is always a middle.

Body Language and Etiquette in Brazil

Here are some examples of body language and etiquette you'll find in Brazil.

Brazilians avoid wearing a color combination of yellow and green. These are the colors of the Brazilian flag.

Brazilians are "high touch"—which means that touching arms, elbows, and backs while in conversation is common. They also stand closer together in conversation and in crowds than North Americans do.

People shake hands to greet. But woman often greet each other by exchanging kisses on both cheeks, starting with the left cheek. Men often greet each other by shaking the man's hand with one hand and grabbing his shoulder with the other.

The hand signal that indicates "okay" (index finger and thumb touching to make a circle) is considered a rude gesture in Brazil. People use the "thumbs up" gesture instead.

A Brazilian may pinch his or her earlobe to express appreciation.

A gesture thought to bring good luck is placing the thumb between the index finger and middle finger while making a fist. This is called a "fig."

Flicking the fingertips under the chin means that the person doesn't know the answer to a question.

Men and women wear full suits in business situations, in churches, and in government buildings. Anywhere else—in shops and restaurants, for example—they'll wear shorts, tank tops, mini-skirts, flip-flops, and other casual clothing. But whatever they wear, they dress nicely!

Brazilians rarely raise their voices or show anger in public.

If you're invited to a Brazilian home, arrive about half an hour late for dinner and about an hour late for a party. Don't forget to bring a small gift such as flowers. But avoid purple flowers (except violets), which are associated with funerals.

38

Know Before You Go

Brazil is the only Portuguese-speaking country in Latin America. Portuguese is similar to Spanish, but the pronunciation is softer. Brazilian Portuguese has been greatly influenced and enriched by the cultures of the South American Indians and African slaves. As a result, Brazilian Portuguese is different from the language spoken in Portugal.

Here are some common phrases you will use in Brazil. The spelling is also given. Try them out, and then look up some additional ones.

English	Portuguese
Hi!	Oi!
Good morning.	Bom dia!
Good afternoon.	Boa tarde!
Good evening/Good night.	Boa noite!
Bye. (informal use)	Tchau!
Thank you. (male/female person)	Obrigado / Obrigada.
You are welcome.	De nada.
Please excuse me (asking for information)	Por favor.
Sorry (apologizing).	Desculpe.
My name is….	Meu nome é ….
What is your name?	Como é seu nome?
It is a pleasure to meet you.	Prazer.

1	um
2	dois (speaking to a man or boy)
	duas (speaking to a woman or girl)
3	três
4	quatro
5	cinco
6	seis
7	sete
8	oito
9	nove
10	dex

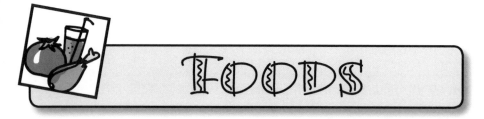

FOODS

Daily Meals

Since the family is so important in Brazilian culture, families dine together at every meal. Sunday lunch is the most important meal of the week. Extended families usually gather on Sunday for a long home-cooked meal that could last a few hours.

Daily breakfast usually includes sweetened coffee with steamed milk, fruit, fruit juice, biscuits or bread, and sometimes cheese or meat. People eat breakfast between 6:00 and 8:30 AM.

In most parts of Brazil, people eat lunch, their main meal of the day, between 11:30 AM and 1:00 PM. Many shops and businesses close for a couple of hours so people can go home to eat. Those who cannot go home eat in stand-up fast-food bars that serve sandwiches like ham with pineapple.

Dinner, which is a light meal unless people are entertaining guests, is eaten from 7:00 PM to 10:00 PM. In big cities like Rio de Janeiro, dinner is later rather than earlier in the evening.

A Blend of Foods as Unique as the Blend of Cultures

The unique blend of cultures in Brazil has resulted in a unique cuisine. Well before the Portuguese arrived, the indigenous people were eating sweet potatoes, corn porridge (a thick, hot cereal), roots, fish, and smoked and dried meats. The African slaves infused Brazilian cooking with traditional African ingredients like spices, peppers, and coconut milk. After slavery ended and immigrants poured into Brazil in the 19th century, foods and recipes common to Asia, Europe, and the Middle East added to the culinary mix. Brazilian cuisine today is a blend of all of these cultural elements. The result is some very delicious dishes!

Foods Common to All of Brazil

Foods universal to all of Brazil are rice *(arroz)* and beans *(feijão),* often flavored with pork or beef. Also on everyone's table is *farofa,* which is toasted cassava *(manioc)* flour flavored with salt, smoked meat, olives, eggs, and spices. It is sprinkled over rice and other dishes to add savory favor.

Since the Brazilian tropical areas produce a wealth of bananas, pineapples, melons, mangoes, and oranges, every meal is likely to include fresh fruit or fruit juice. The dairy state of Minas Gerais is known for its cheese. Brazilians can get any number of cheeses to suit every taste from soft and creamy to hard and salty.

Regional Foods

As in North America, some foods and recipes are more common in certain regions than in others.

The South
The south is known for *churrasco.* This large variety of meats includes chicken, beef, sausage, and pork that is sliced, barbequed, and served with salads. One traditional food from the southern state of Paraná is *barreado.* This meat is made in ceramic pans and often put under the soil to boil with the sun's heat.

The Southeast
Here you will find *feijoada,* the national dish of Brazil. Inspired by the African slaves, this stew is a mixture of black beans with dried, salted, and smoked meats, along with spices and greens. People all over the country have their own special recipe for feijoada.

The Central West
This region is famous for the fish caught in the surrounding waters. It's usually served baked and whole (maybe even with the head and fins left on), with rice and fish broth.

The North
Fish, which was a staple of the Amazon basin Indians who originally populated this area, is a favorite here, too. It is prepared with sauces made of herbs and roots foraged from the local forest.

The Northeast
People in this region enjoy fish near the coast and dried beef *(seca)* inland. The dishes in this region reflect the strong African influence and include many traditional African ingredients like coconut milk, spiced shrimp, hot peppers, nuts, and cilantro.

Other Common Foods

Sweets
Ice cream, custard, and candies *(doces)* are at the top of the Brazilian dessert list. Puddings are popular, too, and you'll find many different flavors. These include *cuscuz branco,* the Brazilian version of rice pudding made with tapioca, coconut milk, and sugar; bread pudding with dried oranges and cloves; and coconut pudding with chocolate and dried plums.

If you like cake, you'll find cakes galore in lots of textures and flavors. Honey cake, carrot cake, corn cake, chocolate cake, cheese cake, orange cake, banana cake with cinnamon—these are just a few of them!

Both kids and adults enjoy dropping into the many *confeitarias* (pastry shops) found throughout the country for a baked treat.

Beverages
Coffee, coffee, coffee! If there is one drink associated with Brazil, it is coffee. Brazilians like their coffee rich—it's about ten times stronger than typical North American coffee. If you're offered coffee in a Brazilian home, expect to be served a very strong brew in a very small cup or a glass. You'll get it with milk for breakfast and black the rest of the day. Either way, you'll get it sweet.

Coffee beans

Fruit juices *(sucos)* are a favorite any time of the day. They're served at the many juice bars throughout Brazil. The typical juice bar drink is a variety of tropical fruits whirled together in a blender. A favorite drink is banana and avocado with milk. A juice bar in a larger city like Rio may offer more than 30 varieties of fresh juice. Coconut juice is a thirst-quenching favorite all over the country. Street vendors just grab a coconut from their cart and open a hole large enough for a straw!

Snacks
Brazilians love to snack any time of the day. Small shops and street vendors sell delicious hot snacks called *salgadinhos.* Here are just a few favorites:

- *pão de queijo*—a small, soft roll made of cassava flour and cheese
- *pastéis*—half-moon-shaped pastries stuffed with a filling
- *empanada*—small pot pies filled with a mixture of chicken or shrimp, palm hearts, peas, and flour
- *coxinha*—a chicken croquette shaped like a chicken thigh

Those who crave a hamburger will find that McDonald's®, the famous American fast-food franchise, is thriving in Brazil. There are now more than 570 McDonald's® restaurants throughout the country.

Pizza is one of the most popular dishes in Brazil, but some of the toppings might be a little unusual to your taste. In addition to cheese, Brazilians might order a "pie" topped with banana and cinnamon, guava jam and cheese, *catupiry* (a spreadable cheese) and chicken, or chocolate! Some people even top off their pizza with mustard, ketchup, or olive oil.

 # Holidays & Festivals

If there is something all Brazilians love to do, it's have a great time! The country is known the world over for its celebrations. Combine this with the welcoming attitude of the people and you have a country that lives for holidays and festivals!

New Year's Day
January 1
Next to Carnival, this is the biggest holiday in Brazil. Since the weather is hot at this time of year, everyone packs the streets for hours of singing, dancing, feasting, and fun.

New Year's in Rio de Janeiro is one of Brazil's premier holiday celebrations. People gather at the beach, wearing white, where multiple stages are set up for performers. It's traditional to burn candles on the beach and launch small wooden boats filled with flowers, gifts, and a wish for the New Year. If the tides carry the boat to the open sea, the wish will be granted.

Along with the candles, white lights sparkle from the city's buildings and from people's balconies. The major hotels host incredible parties that go through the night. A fantastic fireworks display over the water at midnight ushers in the New Year.

Tiradentes' Day
April 21
This holiday commemorates the early movement for independence from Portugal, spearheaded by Joaquim José da Silva Xavier, a dentist called *Tiradentes* (Tooth Puller). Tiradentes was hanged in Rio de Janeiro in 1792, but he is honored as a national martyr.

Labor Day
May 1
This holiday celebrates the achievements of workers and the labor movement. Unlike Labor Day in post-Soviet countries that was once associated with Communism, Labor Day in Brazil does not have any political connection.

Independence Day
September 7
This major patriotic national holiday celebrates Brazil's independence from Portugal that became official September 7, 1822. It is also called the Seventh of September. In typical Brazilian fashion, the celebration is happy and high-energy; it lasts all day and all night. Many people continue to celebrate through the weekend.

Streets are lined with banners and balloons. Thousands of people crowd together, wearing the Brazilian national colors and waving the flag. All major cities host Independence Day parades that draw just about everyone in the city. At night, fireworks light up the skies. In between the parades and the fireworks, there is the typical Brazilian dancing, singing, and feasting.

Our Lady of Aparecida
October 12
The Virgin Mary is much loved in Brazil. This holiday honors her as the country's patron saint. She is represented by a wooden statue of the Virgin Mary in the Basilica of the National Shrine of Our Lady of Aparecida in São Paulo. Pope John Paul II dedicated the Basilica in 1980; it is one of the most visited churches in the world.

All Souls Day
November 2
People honor their departed loved ones by visiting their graves, placing flowers, and lighting a candle. This is sometimes done after a church service when members walk in procession to the local cemetery. Unlike people in Mexico and other Latin countries, however, Brazilians do not have parties in the graveyard on this day. They keep the atmosphere quiet and respectful.

Proclamation of the Republic Day
November 15
This holiday commemorates the Proclamation of the Republic on November 15, 1889 that ended the Brazilian Empire.

Christmas
December 25
The temperature at Christmas in Brazil is very hot, so *Papai Noel* (Father Noel—the Brazilian version of Santa Claus) wears a red silk suit, but he still carries the traditional bag full of gifts. According to folklore, he lives in Greenland and travels to Brazil each year.

One common tradition is *amigo secreto* (secret friend). Maybe you have done a version of this at some point; it is often called *secret pal* or *secret Santa*. At the beginning of December, friends or family members write their name on a piece of paper. The names are then mixed together. Each person takes a paper but doesn't reveal the name of the person on it. All through December, the secret friends exchange correspondence, but they use fake names. On Christmas, the participants gather to reveal their secret friends and give them a special holiday gift.

On December 24, people will go to a church service in the late afternoon or early evening, then gather for supper at midnight. There will be masses on December 25 in the morning and afternoon. Some people prefer to sleep in after the midnight meal or go to the beach in the morning before church. The huge Christmas dinner will include turkey, ham, colored rice, and vegetable and fruit dishes. The day might end with a dip in the ocean to cool off while fireworks and huge Christmas trees of electric lights brighten the skies of major cities like Rio de Janeiro.

One other tradition in Brazil is to set up a *presépio* (a nativity scene) in December. The word comes from the Hebrew word *presepium*—a bed of straw on which the Christ child first slept. The presépio is most common in northeastern Brazil. You'll see them in churches, stores, and in people's homes.

Major Festivals
Carnival (Date Varies)
Brazil is famous the world over for the spectacular street parties of Carnival. This fabulous annual festival begins on the Saturday before Ash Wednesday and lasts four days. With its masquerade balls, parades, singing, dancing, and feasting, Carnival draws people from all over the world.

The preparation for this national event begins months in advance. The level of participation and the costumes vary from one region to the next. In Rio de Janeiro and São Paulo, for example, parades are led by samba dance schools that compete for prizes. The competition takes place in the *sambodromo*, a tiered street designed just for samba parades. Each dance school puts on a spectacular show revolving around a central theme, such as a historic event or a famous person. Sometimes several thousand people from one single club participate.

Cowboy Festival: The Largest Rodeo in the World

The *gaúchos* are the equivalent of North American cowboys. They were skilled horse riders who lived off the land in the 18th and 19th century. The spirit of the gaúchos is very much alive today in the International Cowboy Festival that takes place for several weeks in the southern state of Rio Grande de Sul. Gaúchos from Brazil, Argentina, and Uruguay compete in lassoing, bucking bronco, and roundup events. Many other rodeos are held on ranches in the southern region.

Gaúchos still exist in Brazil. The gaúchos of Rio Grande do Sul wear the distinctive clothing we traditionally associate with gaúchos, including ponchos, billowy trousers tucked into boots, a bandana around the neck, and a wide leather belt with a large buckle. The gaúchos of the northeast, called *vaqueros,* wear hats, coats, and leather chaps.

Gaúcho

Parintins Folklore Festival (June)

This annual festival is second only to the annual Carnival festivities in Rio de Janeiro. Thousands flock to this folklore festival held in Parintins, Amazonas, for three days in June. Often called simply The Festival, the events revolve around the celebration of a local legend about an ox. Two teams compete in retelling this story, trying to outdo each other during a three-hour show with dances, singing, and parade floats before an audience of more than 30,000 people! Other performances are based on Amazonian folklore.

June Festivals

In June, each region of Brazil holds June Festivals *(Festas Juninas)* to celebrate its devotion to the June saints: Saint Anthony (June 13), Saint John the Baptist (June 24), and Saint Peter (June 29). All over Brazil, streets are decorated with colorful banners. People eat delicious foods. Kids play games, have parties, and dress in costume. At night, everyone gathers around soaring bonfires (it's cold in Brazil in June), munches popcorn or corn on the cob, and square dances.

Make a Carnival Mask

The Carnival in Brazil evolved from the African tradition in which villagers paraded through the streets wearing masks and costumes. They decorated their masks with fabric, shells, beads, bones, feathers, and other things that helped show their emotions or helped focus on what they needed. They used feathers, for example, to show their need to rise above illness or problems.

Masks are important to the Carnival costume! Here's how to create your own.

Materials

- piece of cardboard
- pencil
- scissors
- glue
- wooden craft stick
- feathers

- glitter
- sequins
- ribbons
- tempera paints
- brushes
- water bowl, water, and cloth for cleaning paint brushes

Directions

1. Trace the eye mask outline below on a piece of cardboard.

2. Carefully cut out the mask and sections for the eyes.

3. Use any materials on the list above (or choose your own) to decorate your mask.

4. Glue the wooden craft stick to the inside of the mask to use as a handle for holding the mask to your face.

5. What does this mask say about you?

_____

_____

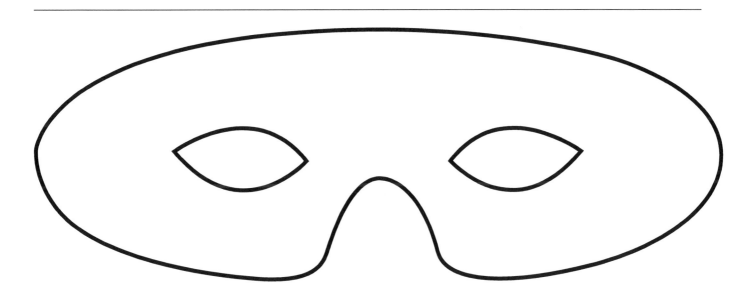

Creative Arts

Music and Dance

The multicultural blend of ethnicities in Brazil has created music and dance as unique as the country itself. Music and dance are at the very core of Brazilian life. After all, what would any great party be without them?

Samba
Samba is the most popular music and dance of Brazil. It's well known all over the world.

Samba originated with African slaves in Rio de Janeiro. Once you hear it, you can't help but move to it! The African influences of the driving beat of the Angolan *tam-tam* (a drum) and rhythmic dance steps make it easy to learn.

Samba was first performed at the Rio Carnival in 1917. The person who made it famous worldwide was Carmen Miranda, star of many Hollywood musicals from the 1930s to the 1950s. She was well known for her costumes—particularly her headdresses filled with fruit. Today there are hundreds of samba schools in Brazil and Europe.

Bossa Nova
The *bossa nova* evolved from the samba and became a worldwide sensation during the 1950s and 1960s. It's quieter and more relaxed than the samba and doesn't rely nearly as much on drums. You may have heard a popular bossa nova song called "The Girl from Ipanema." Although the original bossa nova movement lasted only about six years, it lives on in the many musicians in Brazil, Europe, and Asia who are still inspired by it.

Tropicalismo
Tropicalismo is a Brazilian art movement that began in the 1960s and encompasses music, theatre, poetry, and visual art. But it's primarily associated with music and movement. It's a blend of Brazilian and African rhythms, along with rock and roll. Brazil's military government at the time called the music a threat because the lyrics were frequently political, speaking out against the 1964 military coup in the country. Famous rockers like Kurt Cobain, David Byrne, and Nelly Furtado have said they were influenced by Tropicalismo.

MPB
Tropicalismo has evolved into MPB (*Música Popular Brasileira*), which really means any Brazilian pop music. In MPB you can hear a bit of samba, a bit of folk music, and a bit of rock and pop.

Folk Art

Creating folk art is very much alive in Brazil. In some locales, it's a cornerstone of the local economy. The Indians are increasingly relying on the sale of their crafts because their traditional way of making a living is being destroyed. They bring their wares to folk art fairs regularly held on the weekends to attract the tourist trade.

Certain tribes and areas of the country are associated with various folk arts. The Marajoara, Tapajoara, and other eastern Amazonian Indians are known for their ceramics. The Karaja tribe is known for its painted figures. The Kaxinawa Indians have become famous for their bags and baskets woven from Brazilian leaves, bark, and other natural fibers.

Brazil is famous for its exquisite lace, thanks to the women who originally came to the country from Portugal centuries ago. They settled with their husbands or fathers who were fishermen on Brazil's northeast coast and on the island of Santa Catarina in the south. Today most lace makers are still related to fishermen. In fact, here's a popular saying: "Where there is a fishing net, there is lace." The Renaissance lace made in northeastern state of Pernambuco is the most famous.

Other popular folk art includes jewelry, woodcarving, embroidery, leather goods, and hammocks woven from palm leaves.

Sports & Games

Football

If one thing draws Brazilians together more than their celebrations, it's football (soccer). Football is more than just a game in Brazil—it's a national obsession! Called *futebol*, it's played all over the country, in every social class, just about every day of the year.

Football player

Professional football matches are held in huge stadiums in all of the big Brazilian cities in front of crowds of several hundred thousand people. Famous players like Pelé and Ronaldo are treated like international rock stars. They also become inspirational heroes for kids and adults alike.

There may be strong competition between the local teams in Brazil. There is incredible support for Seleçã, the Brazilian national team. It has won the World Cup (the key international soccer competition) five times (1958, 1962, 1970, 1994, and 2002)!

Auto Racing

Next to soccer, Brazilians love auto racing. The country is producing some world-class championship drivers, particularly in Formula One—the highest class of auto racing, where the cars reach speeds of 220 miles per hour. Three Brazilian drivers have won the Formula One world championship eight times since 1972: Emerson Fittipaldi in 1972 and 1974; Nelson Piquet in 1981, 1983, and 1987; and Ayrton Senna in 1988, 1990 and 1991.

The sport is dangerous, and Ayrton Senna died tragically in a 1994 Grand Prix race in Italy. Brazilians so revered him that the government declared three days of national mourning. Millions of people lined the streets to show their respect. Many improvements in safety standards were made after his death. The children's charities and social programs that his fortune helped to found live on.

Water Sports

With Brazil's thousands of miles of beaches, rivers heavily populated with fish, and lots of waves, Brazilians spend lots of free time doing water sports. Those who prefer to be in or on rather than out of the water enjoy surfing, scuba diving, sport fishing, swimming, and sailing.

If you get to Brazil and want other options for exploring, there are plenty to choose from! Sit on a floating platform in the water offshore, take a cruise to remote fishing villages, buy lunch from a beach vendor, go dolphin watching, ride a dune buggy, play volleyball on the sand, or fly a kite. In short, enjoy yourself! Brazilians do it every day!

Brazil at the Olympics

Brazil has been competing in the Olympic Games since 1920. It has won 91 medals in the Summer Olympic Games, with volleyball, sailing, track and field, and judo the top winning sports. In the fall of 2009, Rio de Janeiro beat out Chicago, Tokyo, and Madrid in winning the right to host the Summer Olympic Games in 2016.

Chile

Atacama Desert
CHILE
Antofagasta
Pacific Ocean
25°
Valparaíso
Santiago
30°
Concepción
35°
40°
Puerto Montt
Chiloé Is.
45°
L. Buenos Aires
Chonos Archipelago de los Chonos
50°
Punta Arenas

PARAGUAY
Gran Chaco
Río de la Plata
Asunción
Uruguay R.
ARGENTINA
Córdoba
Mendoza
Andes Mts.
Buenos Aires
La Plata
URUGUAY
Montevideo
Paraná R.
The Pampas
Mar del Plata
Atlantic
Patagonia
Andes Mts.
N
Stanley
Strait of Magellan
Tierra de Fuego
FALKLAND IS.

0   100   30
0   100   300   5

Welcome to Chile!

Chile is one of the most unusually shaped countries on the planet! But its uniqueness is not limited to its shape. It seems so remote and mysterious. And in some parts of the country, like the vast northern desert, it surely is. Yet, Chile is a modern world leader that has zoomed into the 21st century. It has the most advanced telecommunications system in South America and is one of its key industrialized nations. It is stable and prosperous, and it focuses as much on developing its people as it does on developing its beautiful land.

After you have finished learning about Chile, be sure to check out page 148 for additional classroom activities.

Official Name: Republic of Chile

Location: Southern South America. Chile borders the South Pacific Ocean on the west, Peru to the north, Bolivia to the northeast, Argentina to the east, and the Drake Passage at its southernmost tip.

Population: 16,601,707 (2010 estimate)

Capital City: Santiago

Area: 292,183 square miles. This includes the Pacific islands of Juan Fernández, Salas y Gómez, Desventuradas, and Easter Island. Chile also claims about 480,000 square miles of Antarctica. Chile is slightly smaller than twice the size of the state of Montana.

Major Language: Spanish
German, English
indigenous languages

Major Religion: Christianity (Roman Catholic: 70%)

Currency: The peso   1 peso = 100 centavos (cents)

Climate: Extreme desert climate in the north, temperate in the central region, and cool and damp in the south

The Land: Low coastal mountains; the rugged Andes Mountains in the east; a fertile central valley; a southern coast of inlets, canals, peninsulas, islands, and fjords

Type of Government: Republic

Flag:

The Chilean flag has two equal horizontal bands: white (at the top) and red (at the bottom). There is a blue square in the upper-left corner at the hoist side end of the white band. In the center of the square is a five-pointed star representing a guide to progress and honor. Blue symbolizes the sky, white symbolizes the snow-covered Andes, and red symbolizes the blood that was shed for independence.

Coat of Arms:

Chile's coat of arms is made up of a shield divided into two equal parts. The top is blue, and the bottom is red. There is a five-pointed star in the center of the shield. On the right side of the shield is the condor, a bird of prey from the Andes. On the left side of the shield is a *huemul* (a rare South Andean deer). Both wear a golden crown, which is a symbol of the Chilean Navy's heroic deeds in the Pacific Ocean. The shield is crowned by a crest with a blue, a white, and a red feather—a symbol that former Chilean presidents used to wear on their hats. Underneath the coat of arms and on the pedestal is a white band with the motto "Por la Razón o la Fuerza" ("By right or might").

National Flower: Copihue (Chilean Bellflower)

National Tree: Araucaria araucana (Monkey Puzzle Tree)

National Animals: Condor, Huemul (south Andean deer)

Motto: "By right or might"

Natural Environment

Chile is perhaps the most unusually shaped country on earth, and it is certainly the longest. This slender country, which is often described as a ribbon on South America's southwestern coast, is 2,700 miles long and only 150 miles wide. The country is 18 times longer than its widest point, and its coastline is considered one of the most dangerous in the world. It's no surprise that Chile runs an active lighthouse service all along the coast.

The Andes
The massive Andes Mountains, which stretch 4,300 miles over seven countries, contain 50 active volcanic peaks in Chile alone. The Pacific Ocean is the western border of the country. All along this border are narrow depressions between the Andes and the ocean. The lower slopes of the Andes are covered with grasses and desert brush.

Andean condor

Animals found here include the cougar, the *guanaco* (a cousin to the llama), and the Andean Wolfe. The creature for which Chile is most famous—the Andean condor—soars overhead. It is the largest flying land bird in the Western Hemisphere.

The Atacama Desert
In the north is the Atacama Desert, the driest place on Earth. The desert looks so "otherworldly" that filmmakers have used it as a location for filming scenes that take place on other planets! The Atacama does have rich mineral deposits, however—especially copper. There is a large mining operation here. There are also telescopes in astro-

nomical observatories. The skies are so clear that you can see many things, like the Milky Way, much more clearly here than you can just about anywhere else on earth. Nevertheless, there are few living things in the Atacama—except for cacti. There is virtually no rain.

Central Valley

Most of Chile's population and agriculture is in the fairly small Central Valley. This is also the cultural and political center where the capital of Santiago is located. Here you will find Chilean pine and the beautiful *copihue*, Chile's national flower. Also found here are the numerous crops Chile grows for export, including fruit like apples and peaches, grain crops like wheat and oats, and vegetables like onions and garlic.

Southern Chile

In southern Chile are thick forests with various species of conifers and birch trees, grazing lands, lakes, and a string of volcanoes. In the forests are several types of marsupials and the *pudu*, a small deer. There are also many species of smaller birds.

Chile's indigenous people, the Araucanians, live in the Lake District in the southern part of the country. The southern coast is a maze of inlets, canals, peninsulas, islands, fjords, and glaciers that look like tiny puzzle pieces when you see them on a map. In Atlantic Chile are the grasslands of Patagonia that contain the monkey-puzzle tree, Chile's national tree. It is such an old species that it's called a living fossil.

At Chile's southernmost tip is Cape Horn, which is also the southernmost land in South America. It is at the northern edge of the Drake Passage, the strait between South America and Antarctica. The headlands of Cape Horn are surrounded by almost continually stormy seas.

Humboldt Current

The Humboldt Current is a cold ocean current that flows along the southern tip of Chile to northern Peru. Thanks to the current, the ocean waters off the coast are filled with fish and other marine life, whales, six species of seals, otters, and sea lions. The waterfowl in the area include different types of penguins.

Monkey puzzle tree

The Mysterious Easter Island Moai

Easter Island (in the Pacific Ocean) was annexed to Chile as a special territory in 1888. It is one of the most remote places on Earth. Even if you know little about Easter Island, you've probably seen pictures of its mysterious, monumental rock art called *moai*.

Find a picture of one of the giant stone monuments on Easter Island. Either paste a picture of the monument in the box below or draw a picture of it. Then write a few sentences about what the monument was probably used for or represented. Share what you've learned!

Probable use or symbolism: _____

_____

_____

_____

_____

_____

A HISTORY OF CHILE

Archaeologists think South America was populated by people who walked from Siberia to Alaska across the Bering land bridge as far back as 60,000 BCE. In the 1980s, a child's footprint was found near the south-central Chilean city of Puerto Montt. The footprint is thought to be about 12,000 years old, and it suggests that people may have come to Chile via a route other than the Bering land bridge. The site of the footprint is thought to be one of the oldest sites in the Americas where people might have lived.

Early Inhabitants

Well-preserved mummies of the Chinchorro and Atacameño cultures give us some of the best evidence of early life in the northern Chilean desert. Other cultures left huge *geoglyphs* (drawings on the ground), rock etchings, and ceramics you can still see today.

The famous Incan culture of Peru briefly tried to conquer what is now northern Chile. But the Mapuche (the original people of southern and central Chile who still live in the country) successfully drove them out.

Early Conquerors

In the 15th century, Spain and Portugal were conquering much of Central and South America, expanding their territories and looking for treasure. With their firearms and fighting methods, these adventurers were determined and ruthless.

In attempting to sail around the earth, the Portuguese explorer Ferdinand Magellan discovered what came to be called the Strait of Magellan in 1520. The Strait is a sea route south of mainland Chile and north of Tierra del Fuego. Spanish explorers marched into Chile from Peru in 1535, looking for gold and other treasure. But what they found were hundreds of thousands of indigenous people who were peacefully hunting and farming—people they could use for cheap labor.

Magellan

The real conquest of Chile began in 1540 when Spanish explorer Pedro de Valdivia, who had helped conquer the Incan Empire in Peru, founded the city of Santiago in 1541. (Santiago, in central Chile, is still the country's capital.) The Spanish did not find the gold and silver they were looking for, but in Chile's central valley they found rich farmland. They made Chile part of the Viceroyalty of Peru. Valdivia became Chile's first governor. He rewarded those loyal to him with large tracts of land. Many of these estates (called *latifundios*) remained in Chile well into the 1960s.

The indigenous people fought fiercely against Spanish rule—particularly the Mapuche, who staged a massive uprising beginning in 1553. Valdivia died during this conflict. But by the time of his death, many settlements had been founded and a society was developing.

Spanish Colony

Chile became a frontier colony of Spain with a large army. But the Spanish army spent a great deal of time fighting the British and the Dutch who tried to invade this rich land. A few of them succeeded—at least partially. British explorer Sir Francis Drake, famous for sailing around the world, raided the principal port of Valparaíso in 1578. By the end of the colonial period, Chile's population of settlers under Spanish rule numbered about 500,000.

Early Republic

In 1810, Chile became a self-governing republic under the Spanish monarchy. But the Chilean people soon fought for total independence. This led to warfare with the Spanish until 1817, when Bernardo O'Higgins led an army to free Chile from Spanish rule in the Chilean War of Independence. In 1818, Chile was proclaimed an independent republic. O'Higgins served as Supreme Director of Chile from 1817 to 1823. He is considered one of Chile's founding fathers.

Under O'Higgins, Chile rapidly began to develop its agriculture, mining, and trade. But wealthy landowners in Chile, as elsewhere in South America, remained extremely powerful. They initially supported O'Higgins but eventually objected to paying more taxes on their land. O'Higgins was forced to resign in 1823. He died in Peru in 1842.

As a result of the War of the Pacific (1879–1884), Chile greatly expanded its land by taking vast areas of Peru and Bolivia. This gave it rich deposits of nitrate, a valuable mineral used in fertilizer, which significantly boosted its mining trade. Railroads were built, ports developed, and foreign investors sunk lots of cash into the country. A new working class of miners developed along with the newly rich business owners. Both of them challenged the political power of the wealthy landowners.

Chilean Civil War

President José Manuel Balmaceda was elected in 1886 and immediately began major public works projects like improving hospitals and schools. Nevertheless, the Chilean Congress removed him from office in 1890.

As a result, the Chilean Civil War broke out in 1891 between those who backed Balmaceda and those who opposed him. More than 10,000 Chileans died during this conflict. The Chilean economy suffered yet continued to protect the interests of the wealthy landowners. By the 1920s, the middle class and working class elected a reformist President, Arturo Alessandri Palma. But the Chilean Congress did not support his administration.

The 20th Century

The first half of the 20th century in Chile was marked by an unstable government and an unstable economy. A military coup in 1925 resulted in a dictatorship, a socialist government, and a large number of political parties.

Constitutional rule was restored in 1932, and it prevailed for 20 years. But landowners remained extremely powerful and controlled 80 percent of the prime farming land. About 75 percent of the rural population still depended on them for work and housing.

Eduardo Frei Montalva
Little changed until the 1960s, when Eduardo Frei Montalva was elected president. He initiated major reforms in education, housing, public health, and land ownership. He also unionized the rural farm workers. Many advances were achieved, but his policies threatened the land owners. Others considered his reforms inadequate. There were workers' strikes. At the end of his term, he had not fully realized his ambitious goals for the country.

Salvador Allende
By 1970, the Chilean economy was in bad shape, and unemployment was high. Senator Salvador Allende was elected president. He was a Marxist who believed the government should control the country's businesses. He put Chile's mines, steel industries, banks, and many other businesses under government control. He redistributed land holdings so more people could own land. He put people to work again with government-funded works projects.

Despite all that Allende did to help the country, many wanted him overthrown. This included the U.S. government. The United States had been a large investor in the Chilean copper mines before Allende decided to put them exclusively under the Chilean government control. It also feared Chile's good relationship with Cuba, a country that

had become a threat to the United States. President Richard Nixon put secret U.S. government agents in Chile to weaken Allende's government and support his opponents.

By early 1973, the Chilean economy was crippled. Teachers, students, mine workers, truck owners, and many others went on long strikes. Finally, Allende was overthrown in 1973 by a military coup. A military government led by General Augusto Pinochet Ugarte took control of the country.

Augusto Pinochet

Pinochet was one of the most brutal leaders of modern times. He led Chile from 1973 to 1990, and his regime was filled with terrible human rights abuses. He had thousands of Allende's supporters killed or tortured. Many thousands more left the country before they suffered the same fate.

Pinochet lost the election in 1989 for a second eight-year term as president. He was arrested in London, England, in 1998 for his part in the deaths and disappearances. He died in 2006 at age 91. He never stood trial for his many crimes.

Chile Today

By the late 1980s, the Chilean government was permitting greater personal and political freedom. The country moved to a free-market economy. There are still some state-run companies, but foreign investors can once again put money into the country, and people can once again own businesses. In 2006, Chileans elected their first female president, Michelle Bachelet Jeria. Oddly enough, at one time, she had been imprisoned and tortured under Pinochet.

Chile is now one of the most-developed countries in the world. It has become an exceptionally strong leader among South American countries. Its economy has improved greatly. The new administration is instituting far-reaching social changes. It now supplies one-third of the world's copper and gets record-high prices for it. Thousands of people are immigrating to Chile annually—especially from neighboring countries like Argentina, Bolivia, and Peru—in search of a new life in a stable democratic nation.

Daily Life

The Family Unit

Family is all-important in Chile. Most people live with their families until they get married. Grandparents continue to be parent figures to their children and grandchildren. A grandparent may move back in with a son or daughter if he or she has been left alone because of the death of a spouse.

Married adult children visit their parents frequently, talk to them often, and still ask for their advice. Immediate family members and extended family, like aunts and uncles, all get together regularly and rely on each other for support.

Family roles are still very traditional. A father is the family's authority figure and head of the house. A mother cares for the kids and takes care of the daily activities of running the house. Most middle-class and upper-class families will probably have a live-in nanny to help with child care. Since it's increasingly common for both parents to work outside the home, more businesses are providing child care facilities.

Chilean parents are not strict with their kids. In fact, Chilean kids are treated as equals and are encouraged to stay close to the family for life. They're also allowed to take part in all social gatherings—even if it means going to bed late!

Chilean Homes

Wealthy Chileans live in exclusive neighborhoods in large houses built in a variety of architectural styles. In large middle-class neighborhoods, you'll find smaller American-style bungalows that have been popular since the 1960s. The very poor live in low-income housing within the city limits.

In the country, people live in settlements close to the main roads and highways. They used to live in small adobe houses on the rural estates, but at quite a distance from the landowner's house, called the *casa patronal*. Today you can visit a well-maintained casa patronal in the Central Valley. They have been preserved as tourist attractions to show what traditional rural life in Chile used to be like.

Are We There Yet?

Bus
The bus system in Chile is efficient and inexpensive. There are bus lines in and between towns, and lines that cover the entire country. Ticket prices are usually higher on the weekends and holidays.

People use *La Micro* (which refers to the microbus) to get across town in the larger cities. In Santiago they buy a travel card called "BIP" and charge money to it. They can also use this card to travel on the subway. But a card must be used; money isn't accepted on buses and subways.

Some people use the *Colectivo* to get around quickly. These small cars are a combination of La Micro and a taxi. Fares are very reasonable but will vary depending on the hour of the day.

Metro
In Santiago, Valparaiso, and Conception, the metropolitan railway system (*Metro*) is one of the best ways to get around. People can ride as much as they want in a single day for one entrance fee.

Cars

People do drive cars, but rush hours in the larger cities means road that are packed, especially between 7:00 and 9:00 AM and 5:00 and 8:00 PM. Some cities like Santiago have reverse traffic flow, which means that at certain times of the day, the traffic direction reverses. Parking spaces and streets are narrow, so smaller cars are popular! Driving in between cities is pretty easy because the roads are well maintained. Many of the inter-city roads are toll roads, but not all of the roads have toll booths. Many have free-flow tolling in which the toll is automatically calculated by an electronic tag in the car as it goes under the tolling point. The toll is then billed to the car.

Rural Transportation

The Chilean rural way of life has changed drastically, but some indigenous people still use methods of transportation from days gone by. An "oxen chariot," for example, is a two-wheeled vehicle with large wooden wheels made from tree trunks. Horses, mules, donkeys, and even llamas are used for transportation and as beasts of burden in some parts of the country. People also get around in trucks or on motorcycles and bicycles. In the southern islands, it's simply easiest to travel by boat.

oxen chariot

Going to School

Chileans take education seriously. It is a basic right, according to the Constitution. All Chilean children must attend primary and secondary school. Up to age five, kids can go to preschool. Primary school for kids from five to 13 is divided into eight grades. Kids from 13 to 18 go to secondary school, which is divided into four grades.

All public schools are free. Students wear uniforms to school. But there are few school buses, so kids take public transportation to school, hitch a ride with mom or dad, or walk.

In secondary school, students start choosing their subjects of interest. They can major in science (math, physics, chemistry, and biology) or humanities (literature, history, and sociology). They can also start to pursue a technical-professional education in which they get extra schooling in technical areas, like electronics or mechanics. Students who pursue the technical track can start to work right after high school and save money for further education.

Students who want to go to university can choose between state (public) or private universities. Students who want to go to state schools (and several private ones) take an entrance test similar to the SAT or other standardized test. The student will be tested in math, language, and in the subjects he or she wants to study at university.

Famous Chileans

Two Chilean poets have won Nobel Prizes in Literature. Poet Gabriela Mistral (1889–1957) won the Nobel Prize in 1945. She was the first Latin American to do so. She was a well-known educator and journalist who also represented Latin America internationally.

Poet Pablo Neruda (1904–1973) won the Nobel Prize in 1971. He is one of the greatest poets of the 20th century. Like Gabriela Mistral, he held several diplomatic posts. Neruda's three homes located in Isla Negra, Santiago, and Valparaiso are now museums and open to the public.

Language & Expressions

Here are some fun facts about verbal and nonverbal communication in Chile.

Famous Chilean Proverbs

Here are five famous Chilean proverbs. What do you think they mean?

He who finds not love finds nothing.
One devil that you know is better than twenty you don't.
We all have something of a doctor, a poet, and a fool.
He who is warned in time is saved.
He who divides and shares always takes the best part.

Body Language and Etiquette in Chile

Body language is nonverbal communication. Etiquette is a usually unwritten form of behavior that people in a society are expected to follow. Here are some examples of body language and etiquette you'll find in Chile.

Men rise when women enter the room.

Spreading the fingers, palm up, indicates that the person thinks someone else is unintelligent.

Chileans point with their lips instead of their index finger. They pucker their lips and point in the direction of interest. Moving the lips while pointing indicates a large area.

For formal occasions, people shake hands to greet each other. For informal occasions when people know each other well, they shake hands and hug. Chileans normally give both male and female friends a kiss on the right cheek.

When invited for dinner, Chileans show up about 20 minutes after the agreed-upon time. But they arrive on time for business appointments.

Chileans keep their hands above the table while dining.

People are reserved in public places like restaurants and do not talk loudly.

Slapping the right fist onto the left palm is considered a rude gesture.

Know Before You Go

Very few people speak English in Chile. Spanish is the major language, and Chileans speak it very rapidly. They also use many slang words and idioms known only to Chileans. Check out page 15 for some common phrases you will use in Chile. The spelling and pronunciation are also given. But the pronunciation may sound a bit different when a Chilean says them! You'll have to listen carefully.

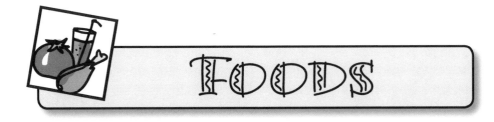

Foods

Daily Meals

Chileans eat four times a day. A meal is not only a good time to eat, it's also a good time for everyone to get together. Chileans eat at home much of the time and go to restaurants for special occasions.

Breakfast is usually light and often includes toast with butter and coffee with milk. Lunch is the main meal of the day. Some businesses close for two or three hours so people can go home and eat with their families and take a nap. Lunch is served between 1:00 and 2:00 PM and traditionally includes two dishes. The first dish is a salad that may be as simple as sliced onions, chopped tomatoes, herbs, and oil-and-vinegar dressing. The second dish is probably beef or chicken. One favorite second dish is *pastel de choclo* (*choclo* is the Mapuche word for *corn*). This corn-and-beef casserole is topped with sugar and cooked in a traditional ceramic handmade bowl called a *paila*.

Chileans have a version of British tea about 5:00 PM, when they'll have bread and jam as well as other finger foods like cheese. Dinner is served late in the evening, around 9:00 PM. This is a single dish but a hearty one like *cazuela de ave*, a thick stew of chicken, potatoes, rice, green peppers, and onions. At both lunch and dinner, *chanco en piedra* (chili and tomato spread) is served with bread.

Common Foods

Favorite National Dishes

Chilean cuisine is a blend of influences from its indigenous people, like the Mapuche, as well the country's European settlers (especially the Spanish). Olives, corn, beans, tomatoes, onions, potatoes, lots of seafood, *quinoa* (a grain crop with edible seeds), beef, chicken, pork, and many fruits are common ingredients. Chilean cuisine is known for its salty, savory flavor and for its colorful dishes. Here are some national favorites:

Porotos granados, Chilean pumpkin and bean stew, has traditional Indian ingredients (corn, squash, pumpkin, and beans) with traditional Spanish ingredients (onion and garlic).

Humitas is a favorite dish that comes directly from Chile's indigenous people. Fresh grated corn is mixed into a paste with fried onions, butter or lard, basil, salt, pepper, and sometimes cheese. The mixture is then wrapped in cornhusks, tied with thread or twine, and baked or boiled.

Seafood plays a big role in Chilean cuisine, including *locos* (abalone), *machas* (razor clams), *erizos* (large sea urchins), and *cochayuyo* (seaweed). A national seafood favorite is *caldillo de congrio*—a soup of conger eel, tomatoes, potatoes, onions, herbs, and spices.

Empanadas are a favorite, especially at holiday time, whether eaten as a snack, an appetizer, or a meal. These delicious stuffed pastries originated in Spain and are either baked or fried. You'll find them all over Latin America, each with a slightly different type of filling. In Chile, a baked empanada is usually filled with ground beef and other savory ingredients like olives. Fried empanadas are filled with cheese. Other fillings include mussels, crabs, and abalone.

Curanto is a traditional food of the islands off the coast of Chile, but people in southern Chile love it, too. This is the Chilean version of a New England clambake. A four- or five-foot hole is dug in the ground. The bottom is covered with stones, and the stones heated with a big bonfire. Then ingredients like shellfish and fish, meat, potatoes, and vegetables are layered in the hole. Each layer is covered with rhubarb, fig, or white cabbage leaves. Then the top layer is covered with wet sacks to help steam the cooking food. The cooked result is delicious!

Curanto

Sweets
Manjar is a brown dessert topping or cake filling made from boiled milk and sugar. It tastes like caramel and is very similar to the *dulce de leche* found in Argentina and other Latin countries. *Alfajor* is a flat, round pastry filled with manjar and covered in chocolate. A *berlin* is a jam-filled donut similar to a jelly donut.

Fruits are popular desserts served sliced, cooked, or made into compote. *Papaya con crema,* for example, is papaya preserves with whipped cream. One dessert that sounds a little more like a side dish than dessert is *mote con huesillo*—dried peaches and stewed corn, cooked together and served as a drink.

Beverages, Snacks, and Fast Foods
Ponche is a popular, tasty punch that includes cranberry juice, cinnamon, nutmeg, cloves, and citrus fruit. It's made by boiling all the ingredients together then letting them cool. Served cold, it's a refreshing drink any time of day.

The humble hot dog is a favorite fast food! Chileans eat them with mustard, avocado, tomatoes, and mayonnaise. Hamburgers (with or without a bun) and other sandwiches are handy snacks. Common sandwich fillings include sliced meat and cheese, diced chicken, tomato, and avocado. You will find McDonald's®, Pizza Hut®, KFC®, and Subway®, as well as Starbucks Coffee® in all of the larger cities. Fast-food restaurants whose names you might not recognize include Fritz (burgers), Pagoda (Chinese food), and Lomitón (burgers and hotdogs). Some restaurants offer "healthy" fast food buffets.

Holidays & Festivals

The Easter Season
Date Varies
For the Roman Catholics in Chile, Easter is a time of reflection and fasting. Palm Sunday, also called *Domingo de Ramos*, takes place the Sunday before Easter. People celebrate with religious services and, in some towns and cities, with processions.

On Good Friday, two days before Easter, people fast and eat fish instead of meat. Radio stations play special "mourning" programs—somber music that reminds people of the death of Jesus. This continues until Easter morning when the resurrection of Jesus is celebrated. In the capital of Santiago and the towns around it, people celebrate with parades and a special church service. Santiago has a history dating back to the 16th century of celebrating a religious fiesta on Easter.

Labor Day
May 1
During this national holiday, workers are honored and people get together for informal barbeques and parties. In Chile, union leaders and government representatives take part in gatherings of workers. Everyone celebrates the importance of the nation's labor force.

Independence Day
September 18
This day of national unity is called The 18th. It is Chile's most important nonreligious holiday. On September 18, 1810, the country declared its independence from Spain. Chileans visit *fondas* (shelters with palm roofs),where they eat traditional foods like empanadas and dance the *cueca* (the national dance). In the days surrounding the festivities, kids fly kites with their families.

The historic figures who fought for Chilean independence are honored. Large *parrilladas* (barbecues) are organized across the country. In many of the special celebrations, you will see people dressed like the *huaso* (the Chilean cowboy) in a flat-topped hat, a poncho, and boots with large spurs.

Armed Forces Day
September 19
Armed Forces Day honors those who serve in the various branches of military services. An extension of the Independence Day celebrations, this day is marked with parades, rodeos, and parties where people dance the ceuca.

In addition to Christmas, September 18th and 19th are the most important days of the year for Chileans. Even though the celebration is officially only two days long, the *fiestas patrias* (patriotic parties) can go on for a week! They're so popular that many businesses and schools close for an entire week.

All Saints' Day
November 1
No matter their religion, most Chileans believe in an afterlife and honor those who have passed away. On All Saints' Day, many visit the cemeteries, leaving bouquets of flowers on the graves of family members and friends. It is also common for people to offer a Catholic mass in honor of the departed every year on the anniversary of the person's death.

Feast of the Immaculate Conception of the Virgin Mary
December 8
The Feast of the Immaculate Conception is a key Roman Catholic holiday throughout the world. Many people from the Chilean capital of Santiago make a *pilgrimage* (a journey to a religious shrine) to the Santuario de la Virgin de lo Vásquez shrine about 50 miles away. Some people show their devotion by walking many of the miles on their knees.

Christmas
December 24
Christmas in the Southern Hemisphere is hot because the seasons are the opposite of those in the Northern Hemisphere. But that doesn't stop Chileans from celebrating a traditional Christmas. Families decorate Christmas trees and put up nativity scenes. The holiday is celebrated more on Christmas Eve than on Christmas. People eat a late meal on Christmas Eve and open presents brought by *Viejo Pascuero* (Old Man Christmas). Special treats enjoyed by all are *pan de pascua,* a Christmas cake made with fruits and nuts, and *cola de mono,* or Chilean eggnog.

New Year's Eve and New Year's Day
December 31 and January 1
These holidays mark the beginning of the summer vacation for many people. At midnight on New Year's Eve, people hug and kiss and say, "Good luck and may all your wishes come true." Some eat *lentejas* (lentils) at midnight in the belief that this brings good luck. There is also a spectacular fireworks display at the port of Valparaíso that is shown on TV. Since the weather is so warm, both days are good times to get together for *asado* (barbeque).

Name Day
Many Roman Catholic Chileans celebrate the saint's feast day with the same name as their own. Name days are treated like birthdays (although people celebrate their birthdays, too). There is a big party, complete with *torta de cumpleaños* (birthday cake). Of course, people will have birthday cake on their birthdays, too!

La Tirana Festival
July 12–July 18
There are many religious festivals in Chile, but the most famous one is La Tirana. The tiny town of La Tirana near the Atacama Desert doesn't even have 1,000 citizens. Most of the year, it's quiet and calm. But between July 12 and July 18, at least 100,000 visitors flock to La Tirana to honor the Virgin of Carmen. She is the patron saint of Chile's *mestizos* (the population in Chile of mixed Indian and European ancestry).

The town is transformed! People play music and wear colorful costumes and masks. Dance companies fill the streets and even the rooftops. The party lasts several fun days with everyone taking a break to enjoy the Carnival atmosphere.

Creative Arts

Music and Dance

Cueca: The National Dance

The *cueca* is the national dance of Chile. People have a lot of fun performing it on national holidays (especially Independence Day), at festivals, and at parties. Basically, this dance reenacts the courting ritual between a rooster and a hen. The male is proud and aggressive; the female is shy and modest. The dancers wave handkerchiefs above their heads to symbolize a rooster's comb or the birds' feathers.

Particularly on Independence Day, cueca dancers will wear the traditional Chilean *huaso* clothing. (See the section on the huaso below.) The man's outfit is a flat cowboy hat, a shirt, a wide sash around the waist, a poncho, riding pants, a

Cueca dancers

short waist jacket, riding boots, and spurs with long shanks. The woman's outfit is a flowered dress with an apron. Sometimes the dance is accompanied with singing, sometimes just with trumpets, drums, and other instruments. Cueca dance competitions are held all over the country.

Frutillar Music Festival

In addition to traditional folk music, Chileans enjoy lots of other types of music, including classical, chamber music, and jazz. A good way to sample the best music in these genres is to go to the Frutillar Music Festival during January and February each year. Thousands attend this important classical music celebration, which is now more than 40 years old.

Frutillar is a lake resort in southern Chile on the shores of the country's second largest lake. It reflects the heritage of its German settlers in its current population, architecture, and food. Singers and musicians from all over Chile have individual concerts both morning and night.

The Huaso

The *huaso* in Chile is similar to the *gaucho* of Argentina and plays the same important part in Chilean folklore. The major difference between the huaso and the gaucho is that huasos are involved in cattle herding and also in farming. Most huasos live south of the capital of Santiago in Chile's central valley where there are a lot of cattle farms. Huasos figure heavily in Chilean folklore. No parade, fiesta, or holiday is complete without them. The huasos are the superstars of Chilean rodeo—an exciting national pastime—especially on Independence Day. Riding their *criollos*, the Chilean horse, they look like they belong to another time!

Huaso

Folk Art

Chileans are widely known for the beautiful folk art they produce for export and for sale locally to tourists. In the north, folk artists weave ponchos and hats from alpaca and llama wool. Chilean rugs, known for their brilliant color, and the traditional brown blanket known as the *ikis* also come from this region.

Central Chile is a key Latin American basket-making region. Key products are bread baskets and placemats. This region is also famous for clay figurines that are generally black and decorated with white geometric patterns. Also created here are guitar cases (the guitar is one of Chile's main instruments), animal-shaped piggy banks, and metalwork.

Mapuche Art

The Mapuche, Chile's indigenous people, lived in southern Chile at the time the Spanish arrived. This is where most of them live today, in their own communities, relatively apart from mainstream Chilean society. About four percent of Chile's population is Mapuche, but many Chileans have Mapuche ancestry.

Mapuches are known for their creative arts, which are generally available for sale to tourists at street fairs. Pottery, primitive baskets made with native plant fibers, and woven garments are just some of the many items they produce. But they are most famous for their handmade silverwork, which they learned from their ancestors and from the Spanish conquerors. One silver piece known all over the world is the *trapelacucha,* a long, beautiful silver pendant for women. The other well-known piece is the *trarilonco,* a headband of silver coins.

Mapuche art is not just a way to make money. It is at the very heart of the Mapuchean way of life. When a member of a Mapuche community dies, for example, a hand-carved wooden statue is placed on the grave. These unique pieces are more than six feet tall.

The Museo Regional de La Araucanía in Temuco, in the Araucanían region of Chile, displays a wide collection of Mapuchean artifacts like instruments. It also has an exhibit that shows the Mapuches' struggle to maintain their culture in the face of the Spanish conquest.

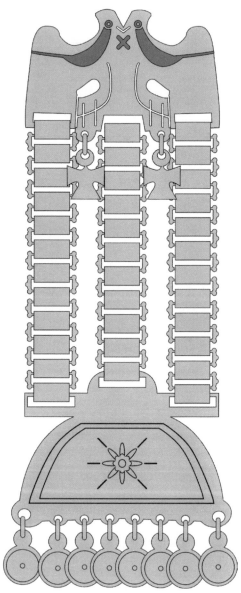

Trapelacucha

Name _____ Date _____

Make a Chilean Rainstick

Once you've heard the sound of a rainstick, you will never forget it! Today they're popular tourist items, but they were once used in many cultures as a way to ask the gods for rain. They are thought to have originated in Chile or Peru.

In Chile, rainsticks are made of hollow cactus tubes with cactus spines inserted in a crisscross pattern inside the tube from the top to the bottom. The tiny pebbles that tumbled through the cactus spines in the tube sounded like falling rain.

Rainstick

Materials
- a cardboard paper towel tube or a long cardboard gift wrap tube
- heavy cardboard or poster board
- 1 cup of uncooked rice, unpopped popcorn, or uncooked beans like lentils
- masking tape
- scissors
- your choice: crayons, markers, colored bits of tissue paper, glitter, feathers, ribbon, rough twine

Directions
1. Trace two circles around the end of your tube onto a piece of heavy cardboard or poster board. Cut out these two circles.

2. Tape one of the circles over one end of the tube. Cover the entire circle with masking tape.

3. Decorate the cardboard tube. Do this with anything you choose: crayons, markers, glued bits of tissue paper, glitter, feathers, or rough twine. You can even consider putting your own personal symbols on it—whatever you like!

4. Pour at least 1 cup of uncooked rice, unpopped popcorn, or uncooked lentils into the tube.

5. Cover the open end with your hand and slowly turn the rainstick from side to side. If you need more rice, popcorn, or lentils to get the sound you like, add some more!

6. Once you're happy with the sound, tape the second circle over the open end of the tube. Make sure the entire circle is covered with tape. Then decorate the circle.

7. Enjoy your rainstick! Consider taking an umbrella if you use it outdoors—just in case it rains!

Sports & Games

Football

Like people throughout South America, Chileans love to play football (soccer). Kids play on both school teams and soccer club teams. You're likely to find kids of all ages kicking around a ball wherever there's even a little open space.

Chile has appeared in seven FIFA (International Federation of Association Football) World Cups and four Copa América (America Cup) competitions, which is the main event of the men's national football teams in South America. It has also won three medals at the Pan American Games and a bronze medal at the 2000 Summer Olympic Games. Thousands of Chileans attend the professional matches.

Rodeo

The people of Chile held their first rodeo (or *la fiesta huasa*) more than 400 years ago, and they have loved them ever since. Huge crowds go to watch them. Rodeo is a much-loved national sport in Chile. It is second only to football in popularity.

But rodeo in Chile is a bit different from rodeo in North America. In Chilean rodeo, the corral is shaped like a half-moon. A team of two riders gallop laps around an arena, trying to stop a calf by pinning it against big cushions. Points are earned according to where the animal is stopped on its body (at the front legs, at the back legs, etc.).

Only the hardy Chilean horse is allowed in Chilean rodeo—no other breed is permitted. Riders must wear the traditional huaso costume of flat hats, brightly colored ponchos, and boots with spurs. It's not unusual to see huasos practicing throughout the countryside at any time during the year.

Other Sports

With its fine horses, it's no surprise that Chile is an international force in polo. In 2008 the country won first place at the World Polo Championship. The country has also earned second and third place medals in previous championships.

Of the 13 medals Chileans have won at the Olympics, four of them have been in tennis (three of them in 2004 and one in 2008). Tennis has also become increasingly popular in Chile as a fun, casual sport.

With its miles and miles of sandy beaches that are easy to reach, nearly everyone in Chile enjoys going to the beach to swim, surf, fish, or just spend some time in the sun.

Go Fly a Kite!

Kite flying is a national passion in Chile. Both kids and adults love to do it. In such a windy country, it's easy to get a kite up in the air and keep it there. In September and October, it's spring in the Southern Hemisphere. It's also windy. On any given day—especially during these two months—you'll see kids and adults flying simple kites in the parks, on the beaches, and in the streets. Cities and towns have even designated safe areas for kite flying in order to avoid accidents.

There are many kite clubs in the country as well as kite-making and kite-flying competitions. It's estimated that about 4 million people fill the skies with brightly colored kites on September 18, Chile's Independence Day.

Design Your Own Kite

Kite flying is a favorite national pastime in Chile. Chileans often design their own kites with their favorite colors or symbols.

Design your own kite using the form below. Color it however you choose. Add symbols or even your initials.

If you decide you want to make your own kite, search "how to make a kite" on the Internet. You'll get several methods for making different kinds and shapes of kites. Use this design as the starting point for decorating your kite.

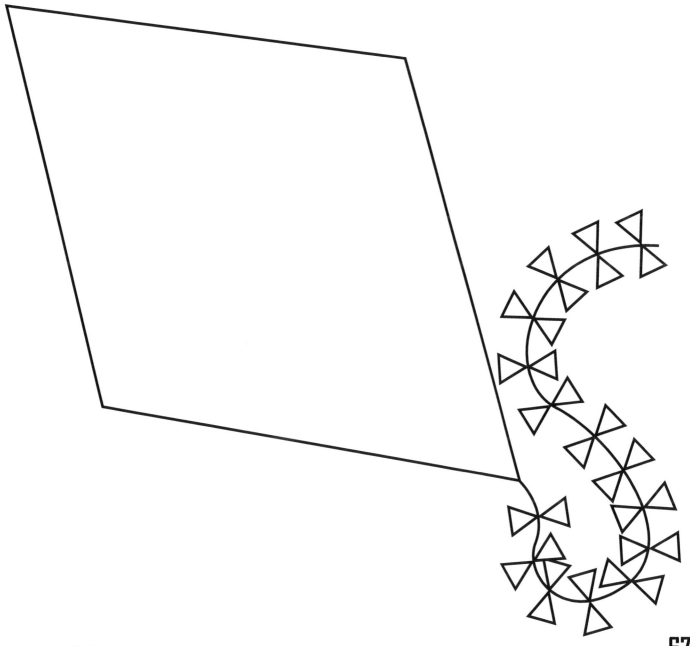

Cuba

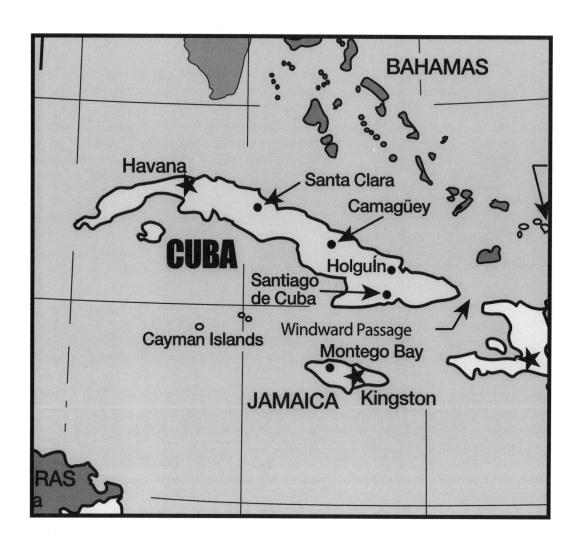

Welcome to Cuba!

Cuba is very close to the United States, yet few people outside of Cuba know much about it. This is due to the iron rule of Fidel Castro. For more than 50 years, Castro was Cuba's dictator, controlling what went on there and what the world was allowed to see. Then, due to ailing health, he transferred power to his brother in 2008. But even though its relationship with world super powers continues to be shaky, Cuba is opening up in many ways. The word *survivor* accurately describes this country and its people.

After you have finished learning about Cuba, be sure to check out page 148 for additional classroom activities.

FAST FACTS

Official Name: Republic of Cuba

Location: Cuba is located in the northern Caribbean, between the Caribbean Sea and the North Atlantic Ocean. The United States lies to the northwest. (Cuba is about 93 miles south of Key West, Florida.) The Bahamas lie to the north. Haiti lies to the east. Jamaica and the Cayman Islands lie to the south. Mexico lies to the west.

Population: 11,451,652 (2010 estimate)

Capital City: Havana

Area: 42,803 square miles. Cuba is the largest country in the Caribbean and the westernmost island of the Greater Antilles. It is slightly smaller than the state of Pennsylvania.

Major Language: Spanish

Major Religion: There is no official religion in Cuba. It was predominantly Roman Catholic before Castro assumed power. Roman Catholicism is still the dominant faith (about 85%), but people do not practice religion openly.

Currency: The Cuban peso   1 Cuban peso = 100 centavos (cents)
The Cuban convertible peso   1 Cuban convertible peso = 100 centavos
(The Cuban convertible peso can only be used in Cuba.)

Climate: Tropical, with trade winds
The dry season is November to April. The rainy season is May to October.

The Land: Mostly flat to rolling plains, with rugged hills and mountains in the southeast

Type of Government: One-Party Socialist Republic (Communist State)

Flag:

The Cuban flag has five equal horizontal bands of blue (at the top, center, and bottom) alternating with bands of white. There is a red equilateral triangle on the hoist side with a white, five-pointed star in the center. The three blue stripes represent the three old divisions of the island. The two white stripes represent the ideal of independence. The red triangle symbolizes equality, fraternity, and freedom, as well as the blood that was shed in the island's struggle for independence. The white star symbolizes freedom.

Coat of Arms:

Cuba's coat of arms is shaped like a pointed shield and divided into three sections. In its upper part, there is a golden key between two mountains and a sun rising over the sea. This scene symbolizes Cuba's position as an emerging state in the Gulf between North and South America. The blue and white stripes down the left side represent the island's division into states in the colonial period. Down the right side is a Cuban country scene with a royal palm tree. This symbolizes Cubans' unbreakable character.

National Flower: Butterfly Flower (White Ginger)

National Tree: Cuban Royal Palm

National Bird: Tocororo (Cuban Trogon). Its red, white and blue plumage matches the colors of the Cuban flag.

Motto: "Homeland or Death"

Natural Environment

Cuba is an *archipelago* (a cluster) of islands in the northern Caribbean Sea where the Gulf of Mexico meets the Atlantic Ocean. Cuba is the main island and is surrounded by four smaller island groups:

- the Colorados Archipelago on the northwestern coast
- the Sabana-Camagüey Archipelago on the north-central Atlantic coast
- the Jardines de la Reina on the south-central coast
- the Canarreos Archipelago on the southwestern coast

The main island of Cuba is 476 miles long and is the world's 16th-largest island by land area. The country suffers a hurricane about every other year during the rainy season. Droughts are common during the dry season.

About a third of the island is mountainous. The Cordillera de Guaniguanico Mountains are in the west. The Escambray Mountains are in the center. The largest system is the rugged Sierra Maestra Mountains in the southeast and south-central areas that are rich in minerals like copper and iron. Turquino Peak, the highest point in the country, is located here. Cuba also has an enormous system of caves. The long coastline of white sandy beaches, coral reefs, swamps, a small river system, and manmade lakes all support the abundant sea life and fisheries.

Mostly, however, Cuba consists of flat to rolling plains. At one time, the island was covered with forest. But much of this was cleared to grow sugarcane, which is still grown in large areas of Cuba today.

Plants and Animals

About one-fourth of Cuba encompasses more than 300 areas designed to protect its plants and animals. This includes six biosphere-reserve areas designed by UNESCO (the United Nations Educational, Scientific and Cultural Organization).

White ginger

About half of the plants found in Cuba are native to the islands and represent about four percent of the total plants on Earth! First, there are colorful tropical flowers. Particularly beautiful are the exotic orchids, the chalicevine with a night-time scent like coconuts, and the fragrant white ginger (the national flower). Several varieties of palm trees are found throughout Cuba—especially the Cuban royal palm (the national tree). The giant kapok tree is also one of the most common of Cuba's trees. It grows more than 200 feet tall and has a trunk up to 10 feet in diameter. It was once considered a sacred tree by those who practiced native religions.

When you think of Cuba's fauna, picture reptiles and amphibians. Cuba ranks 11th in the world in the number of reptiles native to the country. More than half of the reptiles are lizards, like the Cuban rock iguana that reaches four or five feet in length. At the other end of the spectrum is the Monte Iberia dwarf *eleuth*, the smallest frog in the northern hemisphere that measures, fully grown, a tiny 3/8 in. long. Other reptiles and amphibians include the primitive Cuban crocodile (many of which are in Cuba's crocodile breeding centers) and the Cuban boa. The Cuban tree frog is the largest frog species in North America.

Royal palm

Other land mammals, birds, and fish round out the vast array of Cuba's fauna, including some creatures you won't see elsewhere in the world. The Cuban *solenodon* is called a living fossil. This nocturnal, endangered animal looks like a cross between a possum and a mouse with long legs. It has a venomous bite. The Cuban hutia is the largest native mammal in Cuba. *Hutias* resemble a badger or beaver, with stocky legs, long claws, and a waddle-like walk. They live mostly in the treetops.

Cuba's birds are some of the world's most beautiful and colorful. The Cuban *trogon*, the national bird of Cuba, matches the colors of the country's flag. Bee hummingbirds are the smallest birds in the world. They only get up to three inches long, but they can fly 50 miles per hour!

Cuban rock iguana

Finally, the Cuban waters are filled with 57 species of freshwater fish. The primitive Cuban *gar* is thought to be one of the world's first skeletal fish. It can grow longer than 6 feet! Sport fishing for larger fish like bass, tuna, mackerel, barracuda, and swordfish is now bringing tourists to Cuba from all over the world.

Cuban gar

A History of Cuba

Pre-Columbian Times

Of the three major indigenous groups that lived in pre-Columbian Cuba, the Tainos were the most advanced. They farmed the land, growing yucca, corn, peanuts, squash, peppers, fruit, and tobacco. They also sailed the seas. Scientists think they probably traveled the 90-mile distance back and forth to what we now call the Florida Keys.

Spanish Rule

Christopher Columbus, who was exploring new lands for Spain, landed in Cuba on October 28, 1492. He called it *Juana* in honor of Don Juan, Queen Isabella's son. The Spanish eventually came to call the island *Cubanacan,* its Indian name. The Spanish crown commissioned Columbus's son, Diego Velasquez, to conquer and settle Cuba—*and* find its gold and other treasures! By the time Velasquez and his men got to Cuba, they were met with hostile native tribes. But the Spanish overcame the resistance, and the Indians' culture collapsed under their rule.

The Spaniards didn't find much gold in Cuba. But they found a lot of rich farmland. Since there were not enough indigenous people in Cuba to work the land, the Spanish began large-scale slave trading. They shipped African slaves to Cuba to work the coffee and large sugar plantations. Slavery didn't end in Cuba until 1886—more than 20 years after it ended in the United States.

Growth of a Nation

By 1515, there were six small settlements in Cuba. This included Havana, which has been the country's capital since 1607. By the early 17th century, 20,000 Spanish settlers were making their homes—and a very good living—in Cuba. Havana became Cuba's principal port and the naval base for the New World. Most of the ships exploring Central and Latin America stopped in Havana for food and water before returning to Europe.

But Cuba's excellent location made it ripe for attack by European explorers from other countries. The English captured Havana in 1762, but they returned it in 1763 in exchange for Spanish-held Florida.

Cuba's population continued to grow throughout the 18th and early 19th centuries. Thousands of Spanish fled back to Cuba when the British assumed control of Florida. Many fled to Cuba from French Haiti when the native population there revolted and took power. Even more people fled from the Dominican Republic when it was ceded to France. By 1817, the population of Cuba was more than half a million. Havana alone had 70,000 people—more than New York City at that time.

Unsuccessful movements to break with Spain began in 1809 and continued for several years. But Cuba's longest and bloodiest war with Spain broke out in 1868 and resulted in more than 200,000 deaths, lots of property damage (including coffee plantations), and the flight of many wealthy Cubans to Key West. Called the Ten Years' War, this conflict lasted until 1878. It was the first of three wars Cuba fought against Spain in an attempt to gain independence. The second was the Little War (1879–1880). The final three months of the third war, the Cuban War of Independence (1895–1898), became the Spanish-American War.

The Spanish-American War

By the late 1800s, many in the United States were in favor of Cuban independence and were even giving Cuba money to support its struggle for freedom. Due to civil unrest in Cuba, President McKinley sent American Marine

72

forces to the island in 1898 to protect American interests there. He also sent the U.S. battleship *U.S.S. Maine*. The Maine exploded only a month after it arrived; the cause of the explosion is still unknown. But as a result, the United States demanded war with Spain. It also demanded that Spain liberate Cuba.

The war only lasted four months. With the signing of the Treaty of Paris in December of 1898, Spanish rule ended. The Teller Amendment, which the U.S. Congress passed as part of the Declaration of War on Spain, promised Cuba its independence. It also gave the United States the right to have military forces in Cuba.

The Platt Amendment, which replaced the Teller Amendment, established a permanent American naval base in Cuba. Following the Cuban-American Treaty of 1902, Guantánamo Bay Naval Base was built on 45 square miles of land and water in southeastern Cuba. Guantánamo is the oldest overseas U.S. Navy base.

Independence and Struggle

The first Cuban Congress met on May 5, 1902, and began governing the country on May 20. From that time until Fidel Castro assumed power in 1959, Cuba had many presidents and many governments that were mostly made up of military officers or dishonest politicians. Its economy rose and fell.

Cuba experienced its first true dictatorship with the election and re-election of General Gerardo Machado in 1925 and 1928, respectively. During his second term, he declared the military in charge of the government. The Cuban Congress allowed him to suspend basic human rights, such as freedom of speech, press, and assembly. But finally, he was forced to flee the country in 1933.

The Batista Regime

In 1940, Colonel Fulgencio Batista y Zaldívar was elected president, with the backing of the United States. Batista had been the real power behind the country's many presidents until his own election. He was dictator of Cuba from 1933 to 1944 and from 1952 to 1959. During his terms in office, Cuba fought on the side of the allies during World War II. It also established diplomatic ties with the Soviet Union—a fact that would greatly threaten the United States during John F. Kennedy's presidential term.

Batista was overthrown in 1959 as a result of the Cuban Revolution, which had a lot of support from the Soviets. He left the country, paving the way for Fidel Castro.

Cuba Under Castro

Fidel Castro led the rebel army that overthrew Batista and set himself up as Cuban president. During his 50-year regime, Castro controlled all of Cuban life through the Communist Party and the state security police.

Castro first went after the soldiers and policemen of the Batista era. Hundreds of suspects were tortured, executed, or put in prison. He put all newspapers, radio stations, and TV stations under state control. Under a system called the Committees for the Defense of the Revolution (CDR), neighbors spied on each other and informed on those who were disloyal to Castro. Eventually, Castro's government took all property held by religious organizations, including the Roman Catholic Church. Hundreds of priests and other clergy were expelled from the country. The new Cuban government became officially atheist.

Fidel Castro

Castro also put much of Cuba's industry under government control. Many foreign firms in Cuba—most of which were American—could no longer do business in the country. The United States refused to buy Cuban sugar. It also stopped exporting goods to Cuba.

By 1961, Castro's government was firmly backed by the Soviet Union's money and resources. The Soviet Union began to buy Cuban sugar to boost the Cuban economy. And Cuba had the second largest armed forces in Latin America.

In April 1961, just three months after John F. Kennedy became President, the U.S. government invaded southern Cuba in an attempt to overthrow Castro's government. Called the Bay of Pigs Invasion, it was unsuccessful. The Kennedy administration ended up being highly embarrassed by this failure. The Castro regime became even more closely allied with the Soviet Union against the United States.

The relationship between Cuba and the United States was made even worse by the Cuban Missile Crisis. In September 1962, the Cuban and Soviet governments placed nuclear missiles in Cuba. Although the Soviets claimed that the missiles could never reach America, the United States saw this move as the potential start to a nuclear war. After a tense stand-off over several days, Cuba agreed to dismantle the missiles, and the United States agreed not to invade Cuba. But the relationship between the two countries was broken. By 1962, the United States had cut off all trade with Cuba in an effort to bring down the Castro government. Most of these "economic sanctions" are still in place today.

The Soviet Union remained Cuba's great supporter, giving it more than $4 billion annually. It also helped build the Cuban health and education systems and provided military might. But with the collapse of the Soviet Union in 1991, the aid to Cuba stopped. The economy nearly collapsed, and Cubans suffered terribly as a result.

Cuba Today

In 2008, an ailing Fidel Castro said he would not stand for president again. His brother Raúl Castro was elected president several days later.

Raúl has eased some of the restrictions of his brother's regime. People can now have cell phones. They can also buy computers, but only certain people have Internet access. Those who access it illegally face a five-year prison term if caught. The government is looking into loosening traveling restrictions on Cubans. Despite these reforms, Raúl Castro has stated that the Communist government will remain in place.

In 2009 President Barack Obama declared he wanted a new beginning with Cuba. He lifted travel restrictions to the country. Cuban-Americans are allowed to visit relatives in Cuba and send them money. Also being discussed are resuming direct mail service between Cuba and legalizing immigration from Cuba. Illegal immigration to the United States continues to be an extremely serious and life-threatening problem. Each year, several thousand Cubans try to leave the island and enter the United States on homemade rafts, through smugglers, or by using false visas on direct flights to Miami.

Cuba is trading with China, which is investing in the island's nickel industries. In 2009, Cuba's old ally Russia signed an agreement to explore Cuba's offshore oil reserves. Despite these efforts, a great part of the money flowing into Cuba comes from Cubans living in the United States who send their money to relatives at home.

Unfortunately, the hardship and human rights abuses continue in Cuba today. The United Nations has urged Cuba to release its political prisoners and allow freedom of expression. There is no predicting just how long it will take before Cubans are truly free.

Name _____ Date _____

Fidel Castro Timeline

Loved by some and hated by others, Fidel Castro is one of the most forceful figures in history. Use the Internet and other sources to read about Fidel Castro. Choose five to eight key events in his life. Then write them on the timeline below. You can focus on his whole life, or only on events from one particular part of his life—for example, his time as president of Cuba.

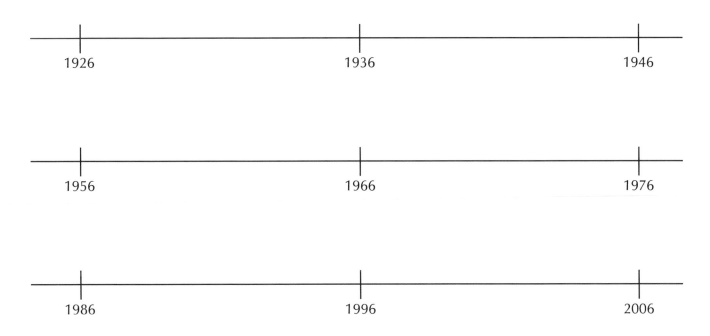

1926   1936   1946

1956   1966   1976

1986   1996   2006

Name _____   Date _____

The Case of Elián González

In 2000, a small Cuban boy was at the center of a big controversy. His name is Elián González. At the time he arrived in the United States from Cuba, he was just seven years old. His custody and immigration status caused heated debate. Many in the United States thought he should be allowed to stay in America permanently. But the U.S. government disagreed.

Using the Internet and other resources, read about the Elián González case and answer the questions below. Then discuss this case with your classmates. Look at the issue from several points of view. How do you think the child felt about his immigration status? How did his relatives in the United States feel about it? How did his father in Cuba feel about it?

1. How did Elián leave Cuba? _____

2. Who was with him? _____

3. What happened during the crossing? _____

4. To whom was Elián released when he reached the United States? _____

5. Why do you think Elián's father did not make the crossing with him in the boat? _____

   _____

6. What did Elián's relatives initially do when the U.S. Attorney General ordered him to be returned

   to Cuba? _____

7. How did the U.S. government eventually remove Elián from his relatives' residence? _____

   _____

8. Where were Elián and his father reunited? _____

9. What did the 11th U.S. Circuit Court of Appeal rule on June 1, 2000, about Elián's right to stay in the

   United States? _____

10. Now that you have read about this case, do you think Elián should have been allowed to stay in the

    United States? _____

Daily Life

Cuba is a Communist country, and this political philosophy affects every aspect of daily life. The government makes decisions about housing, education, health care, and what will be produced in the factories and on the farms. Everyone in the society is considered equal and is expected to contribute to the greater good. Private wealth is thought to contradict Communist principles.

The Family Unit

The family unit is not as strong in Cuba as it is in other Latin American countries. Families tend to be small. The government begins instilling the values of Communism in children at a very early age. Thus, kids are taught at home, in child care centers, and at school to rely on the government to meet their economic and social needs.

Most women in Cuba today work outside of the home. Staying at home to raise the kids is seen as not making an economic contribution to society. Day care centers all over the country free women from daily child care so they can work. But women are still expected to do the housework and take the major responsibility for raising the kids, in addition to having a career. Even though laws passed in the 1970s say that household chores should be shared by both husband and wife if the wife has a job, in reality, this has been hard to enforce.

In addition to the mom, dad, and kids, a typical nuclear family usually includes at least one grandmother. She will help raise at least the youngest children.

Private and Public Space

Most people in Cuba do not own private property like single-family homes or condominiums. Few even have the luxury of living in a large space—most live in very close quarters. In Havana, where thousands of people live and work, there's always a housing shortage, so it's common for families to share an apartment in an apartment block.

Not much new housing has been built in Cuba since the 1960s. The economy has been so bad in rural Cuba that many people have poured into Havana since the early 1990s seeking jobs in the tourism industry. The government has made it illegal for people to live in Havana unless they work there.

Since tourism is slowly being allowed, those who live in tourist areas can rent an extra room to tourists. But the government requires people to pay a lot of money in return for permission to do this.

Since living space is so cramped, it's hard to even have guests in the house, so people often get together on the street in their neighborhoods. This way of socializing in large groups with many other people reinforces the concept of community as family.

Life in rural Cuba remains below the poverty level. People will generally live in one-level houses instead of apartments. But, as in the cities, housing is crowded. People may or may not have access to running water inside the house. As in the cities, people tend to get together outside, whether for a short chat or a community celebration.

Going to School

Education is highly valued in a Communist society, and Cuba is no exception. Cuba provides universal education for kids from preschool through university. In addition to giving students grades, teachers assess both students' and parents' loyalty to Communist ideals. All of this information goes on a student's Cumulative Academic Record. Any negative marks on this record mean the student can be refused a higher education or the right to choose a career.

All children go to primary school. Students who want to attend university and pass the tough entrance exams go to a pre-university that has a difficult academic curriculum. Those who want to have careers in agriculture or industry attend technical schools. Those who get in to university or technical school will have their tuition paid by the government. They'll also receive a monthly stipend for room and board.

Cuban students

Right from their earliest years in school, kids learn that their achievements help the country. They are encouraged to always think about other people's well-being. During high school, kids spend a year away from home doing agricultural work while attending boarding school. This helps them develop an appreciation of working in a cooperative setting. It also provides farm labor.

Military Service After School

All Cuban kids will spend some time in the Cuban army. They usually start preparing for this around age 15 when they join Cuba's Youth Labor Army. Even after they are released from the army and get a job, Cubans remain a "Reservist" until age 49.

Are We There Yet?

Few new cars have been brought into the country since the 1960s. Those that remain are not in great shape. Travel by car is nonexistent—unless it's travel by taxi. Cuban taxis can potentially include unlicensed "yank tanks"— old, big American cars from the 1950s.

"Yank tank"

There are a few bus lines in Cuba that offer differing levels of service. Buses are usually packed, with long lines of people waiting to board. Víazul is a long-distance bus tour line with modern coaches and limited 24-hour service, but few Cubans with an average income can afford the fare. The older bus line, Astro, has a much more extensive network of stops and cheaper fares that the average person can afford. In the provinces, there are very old European buses. Most of them aren't in good shape and they break down a lot, but the fare is the cheapest of all!

Most people both in the city and in the country simply get around by bicycle. In the city, you will even see some horse-drawn carriages. In the country, people still ride oxen, donkeys, or mules.

Famous Cubans

Desi Arnaz (1917–1986), a famous musician and actor, was born in Cuba to a wealthy family. He and his family were forced to flee to Miami during the Batista regime. Arnaz is best known for playing Ricky Ricardo on the TV series *I Love Lucy*. His real-life wife, Lucille Ball, also starred in the series. *I Love Lucy* still airs all over the world in many languages.

Arnaldo Tamayo Méndez (1942–), born in Guantánamo, was the first Cuban cosmonaut. He was also the first person from a country in the Western Hemisphere (other than the United States) to orbit the earth.

Andy García (1956–) was born in Havana. This popular actor has appeared in many of Hollywood's top films, including *The Godfather: Part III, The Untouchables,* and *Ocean's Eleven* and its two sequels.

Daisy Fuentes (1966–) was born in Havana. A popular international TV personality, she is MTV's first Latina VJ. She is also the Revlon cosmetics company's first Latina spokesperson to have a worldwide contract.

Eva Mendes (1974–) is an American actress born in Miami to Cuban parents. She has starred in a number of American films, including *2 Fast 2 Furious* and *Hitch*. She is also an international spokesperson for the Revlon cosmetics company.

Language & Expressions

Here are some fun facts about verbal and nonverbal communication in Cuba.

Famous Cuban Proverbs

Here are six famous Cuban proverbs. What do you think they mean?

When the sun rises, it rises for everyone.
Believe only half of what you see and nothing of what you hear.
Life is short, but a smile takes barely a second.
Listen to what they say of the others, and you will know what they say about you.
A lie runs until it is overtaken by the truth.
Love is like war—easy to begin and hard to end.

Body Language and Etiquette in Cuba

Here are some examples of body language and etiquette you'll find in Cuba.

Cubans are not shy about showing physical affection in public. They will touch each other often in conversation.

It is considered okay to argue about issues in public. However, it is not considered okay to make direct accusations to other people.

Being generous and hospitable is a big part of the culture. Doors are left open, houses and other structures are not fenced in, and visitors are always welcome.

It is polite to greet every man with a handshake and every woman with a kiss on the cheek.

People do not criticize the government or the country's leaders in public.

When visiting a Cuban's home—especially if you stay for more than a day—it is considered polite to give gifts such as towels and linens or toys for the kids. But the cost of the gift is kept fairly low.

It is not considered rude if a person interrupts you while you are speaking. But it is considered rude to look away from a person while you are speaking.

Men stand when a woman enters the room or leaves the table.

It is considered rude to blow your nose or spit in public! It is illegal to litter.

Showing up late to a party or other occasion is common. Cubans may even keep foreigners waiting for up to an hour before starting a business meeting.

Know Before You Go

Check out page 15 for some common phrases you will use in Cuba. The spelling and pronunciation are also given.

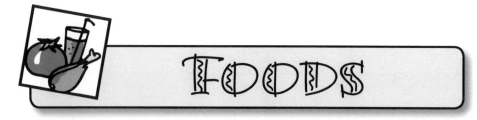

FOODS

A Simple Cuisine

Cuban food is a combination of Spanish, African, and Caribbean cuisine. But compared to the savory dishes of other Latin American countries, it is simple and rather bland. Rice and black beans are on most dining tables every day. *Plantains* (a starchy banana) and potatoes follow close behind. Salads are simple—maybe some chopped cabbage and avocado with vinegar-and-oil dressing. Garlic and onion are the main spices used. Many foods are fried in olive oil or lard.

Pork and chicken are the common meats. Some people raise and slaughter their own pigs and eat most parts of it. (*Chicharones,* for example, are deep-fried pieces of pig fat. They are one of Cuba's most popular snacks.) Beef and fish are not available to the average Cuban because they're sold to expensive resort hotels.

Food Shortages
After the Cuban Revolution, Cuba depended on the Soviet Union for a large part of its food supply, including grain to feed livestock. But the collapse of the Soviet Union in 1991 cut off Cuba's food aid and caused severe food shortages in the country. Since most of Cuba's farmland is given over to sugar cane, tobacco, and tropical fruit for export, the country cannot raise enough food for its people. Cuba imports some foods from Russia, Spain, Portugal, and even the United States. But there is still a shortage. The Cuban government refuses offers of food aid from the United Nations.

Food Rationing
As a result of the food shortages, Cuba has a food rationing system. People's ration books determine how much rice, sugar, beans, potatoes, bread, eggs, meat, fish, cooking oil, and other goods they can buy each month at ration stores.

Vegetables and fruit cost a lot of money, and they're usually hard to get. A pineapple, for example, may cost only a nickel, but the average Cuban only earns from $8 to $35 a month. So, most people don't have the money to buy more than a few fruits and veggies at one time. Since many people don't have good refrigerators (or they experience frequent power outages), the food must be eaten quickly. Foods that can last a little longer like pizza and bread may be cheaper, but they can really pack on the calories. Thus, due to lack of availability and high cost, many people aren't getting enough of the best foods for a balanced diet.

Daily Meals

Breakfast in Cuba is the lightest meal. It may include a piece of grilled bread and coffee with warm milk. But many Cubans skip breakfast because they can get free meals at work and at school. At school, kids are given special cookies that have vitamins and minerals in them to help supplement their diet.

Lunch traditionally includes a simple stew or meat sandwiches with pickles and mustard and a side dish of fried potatoes.

Most Cubans eat the majority of their daily food later in the day after work. The basis for the meal will be fried meat (like chicken), white rice, black beans, fried plantains, and a simple salad.

National Dishes

Cuba's two famous dishes are *ropa vieja* and *picadillo*. Ropa vieja is Spanish for *old clothes*. This popular stew is shredded meat in a tomato sauce served on rice. Picadillo is made with ground meat, tomatoes or tomato sauce, olives, and black turtle beans. It is also served with rice.

Street Food, Sweets, and Soft Drinks

In many cities and towns, street stalls offer cheap, homemade food that people grab for quick snacks. Favorites include tamales, corn fritters, pizza, pies, candies made from shredded coconut, and shortcake cookies called *torticas*. Numerous coffee stands in the town centers offer strong coffee with sugar.

Cuba is a sugar-producing country, and there are many delicious sweets and desserts available. Cake and ice cream top the list. Big pieces of sponge cake topped with meringue are popular—especially for kids' birthday parties. This cake is so important that the government will even supply it for parties if people cannot afford to buy it.

Ice cream is a passion in Cuba. Coppelia, Cuba's national ice cream manufacturer, is famous for its fruit-flavored ice creams.

Finally, soft-drink lovers can get their fill of canned drinks like Coke and Pepsi in many of the local shops. Cuba also has its own brands of lemonade (Cachito), cola (Tropicola), and orangeade (Najita). Other beverages include a fizzy malt drink called Malta and a sweet, spicy drink called Prú.

Dining Out

Unlike most other major countries, there are no fast-food chains in Cuba like McDonald's® or Burger King®. There is, however, a fast food chicken chain called El Rápido. A burger chain called Burgui also has many outlets in the major Cuban cities.

Most Cuban restaurants are owned by the government and are known for slow service and pretty average food. Better food is found in privately-owned restaurants called *paladares*. But the government strictly controls the paladares and forbids them to sell locally-caught shrimp and lobster. These seafood treats are sold to the expensive tourist hotels, along with better meats like beef.

Holidays & Festivals

Many of Cuba's public holidays celebrate important events in the country's history and struggle for independence. People usually head to the beaches for some time off in the sun!

There are no public celebrations in the streets on traditionally religious holidays like Christmas, but people do observe religious holidays privately. They may even have an altar in their homes. The cathedrals in Santiago and Havana continue to hold services, but these are contained strictly within the church walls.

New Year's Eve and Triumph of the Revolution
December 31 and January 1
On New Year's Eve, family and friends gather together for a big meal. At the stroke of midnight, each person eats 12 grapes (one for the memory of each month of the past year).

January 1 is not only the beginning of a new year; it is also Cuba's most celebrated holiday. It honors the Cuban Revolutionary movement that includes the events of 1959 when Batista was overthrown and Castro's forces took over the government.

Carnival
Summer (July in Santiago; Other Dates Vary by Region)
All Central and Latin American countries have Carnival, which is one giant street party before the somber season of Lent. Since Cuba does not openly observe the religious significance of holidays, its Carnival celebrations officially have no religious meaning. But there was Carnival in Cuba way before the Revolution! You'll find the biggest Carnival celebrations in Santiago and Havana, but each region has its own Carnival celebration on its chosen dates.

Carnival

In Havana and Santiago, each neighborhood organizes a performing group that rehearses for months to take part in the Carnival parade and dance show. Bizarre and colorful costumes, dance and music, outdoor street fairs and concerts, and lots of food all are highlights of Cuba's biggest Carnival celebrations.

Santiago's Carnival is the oldest and most famous in Cuba. The Museo del Carnaval in Santiago exhibits lots of items from Santiago's Carnivals. Here you can see old costumes, photos, huge papier-mâché masks, instruments, and recent winners of the Carnival costume contests. You can also enjoy live music and dance performances most days of the week.

Labor Day
May 1
This day honors the nation's workers. Everybody gets the day off. Thousands of people, waving the Cuban flag, crowd into the Plaza de la Revolución in Havana to watch military parades and listen to speeches.

Independence Day
May 20
This holiday celebrates two key events of liberation. First, Carlos Manuel de Céspedes, a sugar cane plantation owner, freed his slaves in 1868 and started the independence war against the Spanish government of Cuba. This holiday also celebrates Cuba's independence from the United States in 1902.

Cubans all over the world celebrate on May 20. In Cuba, there are parades and laying of wreaths at the monuments of Cuban war heroes. Those who have escaped Cuba honor the long and continuing struggle for freedom that people still living in Cuba face every day. They will often hold events and exhibits to highlight the plight of political prisoners and Cubans who have fled the country.

Revolution Anniversary
July 25–July 27
Several days in July commemorate the Cuban Revolution. July 26 honors the day in 1953 when a small group of revolutionaries, led by Fidel Castro, attacked government troops at the Moncada Garrison. This date marks the beginning of the Cuban Revolution. It was also the beginning of the end for President Fulgencio Batista's regime in Cuba and opened the way for the Castro regime.

Day of Cuban Culture
October 10 (several days)
Various communities will celebrate Cuba's culture in their own ways. These include showing films, performing plays, and celebrating the birthdays of national heroes.

Christmas Day
December 25
For many years after the Cuban Revolution, Christmas was just another day. However, the holiday was reinstated in 1998 after Pope John Paul II visited Cuba.

People who celebrate Christmas will do so quietly and in their own way. But it is traditional for Cubans to eat a big dinner on Christmas. A typical meal might include olives, ham spread or ham *croquettes* (a fried caked filled with chopped ham), salad, black beans, mashed plantains, bread, potatoes, white rice, and roasted pig. Dessert might include rice pudding, coconut *flan* (creamy custard), delicious three-milk cake, Christmas cookies, and Cuban eggnog.

Creative Arts

Support for the Arts in Cuba

One of the goals of the Cuban Revolution was to develop every citizen's talents. Thus, the Cuban government supports promising writers, artists, 21 art schools, the Cuban Film Institute, the National Cultural Council, the National School for the Arts, the National Ballet of Cuba, and many other cultural organizations.

The government also makes cultural events affordable for the masses. Most towns have a House of Culture (*Casa de Cultura*) where people can go to hear classical music, see art exhibits, or attend poetry readings and other cultural events. The cost of all cultural events is kept very low so people on an average income can attend.

Music and Dance

Music
Mostly of Spanish and African origin, Cuban music and dance are woven into the fabric of daily life. Any occasion—Carnival, parties, an evening of talking to neighbors in the street—is a good time for music and dance. Traditional instruments are the guitar (the Spanish contribution) and lots of percussion instruments like conga drums and maracas (the African contribution).

Most towns in Cuba hold weekly musical performances in the town plaza. Local groups and orchestras give at least one free concert each weekend. Many towns also have a House of Song (*Casa de la Trova*). These are government-supported social clubs where people go to play and hear traditional Cuban music, and they fill up every night! The best-known House of Song is in Santiago, where many famous traditional Cuban musicians have played. It's open day and night.

Dance
Salsa is the most popular Cuban music and dance genre that is now famous all over the world. It was primarily developed in the 1960s and 1970s by Cuban and Puerto Rican immigrants in New York City, but it soon spread to all of Latin America. Some call it the "pulse" of Latin music.

Ballet

Cuba also embraces classical dance. The country is known worldwide for the National Ballet of Cuba, which is based in Havana. The founder and director, Alicia Alonso, was a great supporter of Castro's Cuban Revolution. As a result, the ballet company receives considerable government funding. The costs of attending the performances are very low (about 25 cents), so all can attend. Each year the National Ballet hosts the International Ballet Festival of Havana, which features dance companies from around the world.

The National Ballet searches the country each year for gifted students who must then qualify to attend the Cuban National Ballet School. Kids from all over Cuba hope to get a spot at the School. Those who go on to dance in the National Ballet can expect to receive an above-average income, government funding, and the opportunity to travel the world. There are more than 4,000 students in the school!

Street Art

As for art in Cuba, many Cuban artists have taken it to the streets! Perhaps nowhere else in the world can you see as much fascinating artwork just about everywhere—on fences, on buildings, and on walls. In every city and town, many drab buildings have been brightened up with bold murals. They don't last long because the sea air destroys them, but the artists then paint new images. You'll see anything from famous revolutionary Che Guevara, animals, pictures that comment on the political situation, or artistic graffiti.

In addition to street art, there is a thriving art scene in Cuba. Each province of Cuba has at least one art school. The Cuban Cultural Fund gives a lot of support to art school graduates. It advertises the artists' work, helps them arrange gallery shows, ships their work, and prints catalogues for the shows. The government now allows some artists to sell their work in other countries.

Film

Cubans love going to the movies, and they only have to pay about 15 cents per ticket to see one. The Cuban film industry has been popular since the late 1950s. Like the media, the film business is owned and subsidized by the government. Each year Havana hosts the Havana Film Festival that promotes the work of Latin American filmmakers and films that have Latin American themes. Throngs of people go from one theater to another, right alongside famous directors, actors, and film producers. There are also lots of cultural events, like book signings and concerts. Many people in Havana save up their vacation time to view some 15 films!

More than 100 films are selected to be shown at the festival and compete for the top prize in several categories. One of the most popular categories is "Made in Cuba"—films about Cuba made by local and foreign filmmakers.

Cuba's Famous and Favorite Shirt

If there is one item of traditional clothing most closely associated with Cuba, it's the *guayabera* (also called the Havana shirt or the Mexican wedding shirt). You'll see people wearing this all over Latin America, and there is some debate about where it originated. The story goes that it was originally made in Spain for a wealthy Cuban rancher in the 1700s. Nevertheless, this cool cotton shirt with beautiful embroidery is part of the national Cuban costume.

Old Havana

Guayabera shirt

Old Havana is such a cultural treasure that it is a UNESCO World Heritage site of cultural significance. To walk through Old Havana is to step back in time. The Cuban government is now restoring the gateways, monuments, forts, churches, palaces, and many other structures that help this area maintain its charm. Buildings in baroque and neoclassical architectural style line the narrow streets and surround the courtyards. The Great Theater of Havana and Morro Castle that guards the entrance to Havana Bay are two of the incredible structures.

Morro Castle

Make Your Own Maracas!

Maracas are one of Cuba's native instruments. These Latin percussion instruments are traditionally made of a hollow gourd with pebbles or beans inside. Essentially, they're rattles that make a fun, swishy sound. Musicians always play two (or even more) of them at a time. The directions below tell you how to make one maraca, but consider making two!

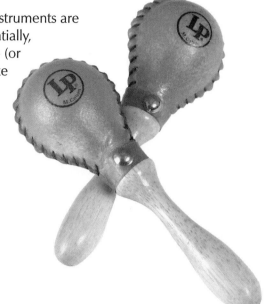

Materials

- funnel
- measuring cup
- ½ cup of small uncooked beans
- 1 balloon
- cardboard tube (such as a tube from gift-wrap roll or a toilet paper tube)
- tape
- scissors
- newspaper
- 2 cups of water
- 2 cups of flour
- regular or fluorescent tempera paints
- paint brushes
- water bowl, water, and cloth for cleaning paint brushes
- glue and glitter (optional)

Directions

1. Insert the funnel into the balloon, and then pour the beans into the balloon.
2. Blow up the balloon to about the size of a grapefruit. Be careful—don't swallow any beans!
3. Tie the balloon in a knot.
4. Make lengthwise cuts about one-half inch apart on the end of the cardboard tube. You'll end up with a tube that has a "fringe" on the bottom of it.
5. Tape the cardboard tube to the underside of the balloon so the tube forms a handle.
6. Stuff newspaper into the cardboard tube. Tape the end of the tube shut.
7. Mix the water and flour together until the mixture is a smooth papier-mâché.
8. Dip strips of newspaper into the papier-mâché and cover the entire balloon and cardboard tube. It's best if you criss-cross the newspaper strips.
9. Let the maraca dry thoroughly.
10. Decorate your maraca with paint and/or glue and glitter.

Sports & Games

The Government's Role in Sports

By law, all Cubans have the right to participate in physical education and organized sports—both of which are incorporated into school programs. INDER (the National Institute of Sport, Physical Education, and Recreation) carries out sports programs for the masses.

From grade school through university, physical education and sports programs are mandatory. Today more than a million kids in Cuba take part in a sport and are tested on their progress during the year. Early each morning, school kids gather in parks, town squares, or school yards to start their day with group physical exercise. They'll play sports later on in the day.

Creating Winners

The kids who show athletic talent by age seven or eight will attend an exclusive School for Sports Initiation. (There is one in every Cuban province.) They'll continue their studies until age 15 or 16 while training intensively in a specific sport. They'll have the benefit of some of the world's best athletic coaching, testing, and facilities. (The Cuban coaches are so well respected that they work with athletes in other countries, particularly in Latin America.) Students will compete with kids from the sports schools in other provinces.

The best students then go on to the even tougher School of Higher Athletic Performance. If they make it to the National Team, they are so fit and well trained that they're ready for Olympic-level competition.

Cuba at the Olympics

Since the 1976 Montréal Olympics, Cubans have been among the top 12 in the medal tables of the Summer Olympic Games. (Cuba does not compete in the Winter Olympics.) Of their total 194, 67 have been gold, with boxing and track and field topping the list. Their best performance to date was the 1992 Barcelona Olympics with 14 gold medals and placing fifth in the final ranking.

Some of the Cuban Olympic athletes have set incredible records. Alberto Juantorena was the only man in Olympic history to win both 400-meter and 800-meter events (Montreal, 1976). Félix Savón took home gold medals in boxing three Olympic Games in a row (Barcelona, 1992; Atlanta, 1996; Sydney, 2000). In Athens in 2004, Cuban boxers took home eight medals (including five gold medals). Javier Sotomayor is considered the best high jumper of all time. He took the gold medal in Barcelona (1992) and the silver medal in Sydney (2000).

Cubans have been world champions in many other competitions. These include the Central American and Caribbean Championships and the Pan American Games.

Sports for the Masses

Baseball

Baseball is the most popular game in Cuba *and* the official sport. It came to the country via American sailors in the 19th century. Today it's common for both boys and girls to play a quick game in the streets or in the school yard.

The Cuban National Baseball Team is currently ranked #1 in the world. It is an amateur team (there are no professional sports team in Cuba), so it can compete in the Olympics. Since 1992, the team has won three Olympic gold medals, along with numerous gold medals in other competitions like the Pan American Games.

Boxing

Amateur boxing is not only a popular spectator sport; it has given Cuba its reputation as a leading international force in this field. Sixty-three of Cuba's 194 Olympic medals are in boxing. It consistently gets medals in major international competitions. Many of Cuba's fighters go on to have professional careers in the ring.

Boxing

Games

Table games like chess and dominoes are popular in Cuba. It's common to see locals, sitting street-side, having a match. In Bayamo, the capital of Cuba's Granma Province, every Saturday night is a big street party. Rows of chess and domino players line the streets, while the neighbors eat homemade snacks, play music, and dance well into the night.

Nicaragua

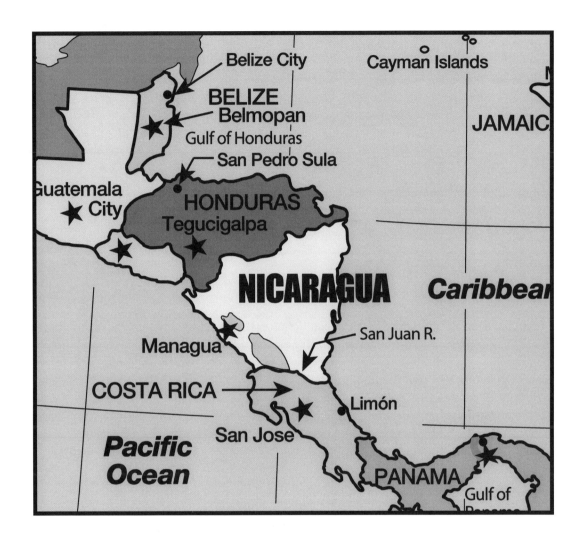

Welcome to Nicaragua!

Nicaragua is the largest country in Central America. Known as the land of lakes and volcanoes, it sits between Honduras and Costa Rica. It's hard to believe that this nature lover's paradise has survived dictatorship, civil war, and terrible natural disasters.

Nicaragua may be the second-poorest nation in the Western Hemisphere, but it is rich in its proud, passionate people and its spectacular landscape. From the rainforest to the beaches—and everywhere else in between—it is incredibly beautiful and peaceful.

After you have finished learning about Nicaragua, be sure to check out page 148 for additional classroom activities.

FAST FACTS

Official Name: Republic of Nicaragua

Location: Central America between Costa Rica on the south and Honduras on the north. Nicaragua borders the Caribbean Sea on the east and the North Pacific Ocean on the south and west.

Population: 5,891,199 (2010 estimate)

Capital City: Managua

Area: 50,193 square miles. Nicaragua is the largest country in Central America. It is slightly smaller than New York state.

Major Language: Spanish 97.5% (the official language)
English and indigenous languages on the Atlantic coast

Major Religion: Christianity (Roman Catholic: 58.5%; Evangelical: 21.6%)

Currency: The córdoba   1 córdoba = 100 centavos (cents)

Climate: Tropical in the lowlands and cooler in the highlands

The Land: Extensive Atlantic coastal plains that rise to interior mountains in the center of the country; narrow Pacific coastal plain interrupted by volcanoes

Type of Government: Republic

Flag: The Nicaraguan flag has three equal horizontal bands of blue (starting at the top), white, and blue. The national coat of arms is centered in the middle white band.

Coat of Arms:

Nicaragua's coat of arms features a triangle encircled by the words REPUBLICA DE NICARAGUA on the top and AMERICA CENTRAL on the bottom. The five volcanoes represent the original five member states, the Cap of Liberty represents national freedom, and the rays of the sun and the rainbow symbolize a bright future.

National Tree: Sancuanjoche (a flowering tree called Frangipani)

National Animal: Turquoise-browed Motmot (a colorful bird)

Motto: "In God We Trust"

Natural Environment

Nicaragua comprises three geographic regions: the Pacific Lowlands in the west, the North-Central Highlands, and the Caribbean Lowlands in the east. The entire country is a nature lover's paradise. Its protected areas, reserves, and rainforests abound with wildlife.

Pacific Lowlands
More than half of Nicaragua's population lives in the Pacific lowlands. The capital of Managua is located here, too. In the broad, hot lowland plains, there are several large volcanoes of the Cordillera Los Maribio Mountain Range, including the active Mombacho and Momotomba.

Mombacho Volcano Nature Reserve is one of Nicaragua's 78 protected areas. Mombacho is a popular tourist spot for those who can make the steep climb up a rugged trail to the cloud forests and dwarf forests. Once there, they get a breath-taking view of Lake Nicaragua and a close look at exquisite orchids.

Western Nicaragua is located where two major tectonic plates collide, so it experiences earthquakes and volcanic eruptions. While the volcanic eruptions cause agricultural damage, the earthquakes have been far more deadly and damaging. The area gets hundreds of earthquakes each year. The capital of Managua has been destroyed twice, most recently in 1972.

North-Central Highlands
About a quarter of Nicaragua's crops, like coffee, are grown in the cooler climate of the North-Central Highlands, particularly on the western slopes. The eastern slopes are covered by rainforests and have little population except for small villages of indigenous people.

As in the Pacific Lowlands, orchids are found in this region's beautiful cloud forests. Colorful birds abound, including exotic toucanets, hummingbirds, goldfinches, and the spectacular resplendent quetzal.

Toucanet

Caribbean Lowlands
The Caribbean Lowlands comprise a large tropical rainforest that makes up about seven percent of the area in Nicaragua. Few people live in this relatively untouched and hot and humid land. It is irrigated by several large rivers, including the Rio Coco that forms part of the border with northeastern Honduras. There are lagoons and deltas all along the coastline, which is called the Mosquito Coast.

During the rainy period from May through October, the Caribbean Lowlands get up to 250 inches of rain annually from tropical storms; sometimes serious flooding results. The Caribbean coast also gets damaging hurricanes, like Hurricane Joan that caused $1 billion in damage in 1988.

The entire area is filled with birds such as eagles, toucans, turkeys and macaws, as well as animals like monkeys, anteaters, deer, and the pig-like tapir.

The Bosawás Biosphere Reserve in the northern part of the Lowlands is a UNESCO biosphere reserve that protects about 1.8 million acres of the tropical Mosquitia Forest. Bluefields, the only major city in this area, is Nicaragua's key Caribbean port where hardwood and seafood are exported. More people here speak English than in the rest of the country.

Major Lakes

Lake Managua in the south is one of the country's largest lakes. The capital city of Managua is on its southwestern shore. Unfortunately, Lake Managua has been severely polluted by industrial waste and decades of sewage being dumped into the lake. (Some people still live here, however, and they eat the fish.)

Lake Managua is joined by the Tipitapa River to Lake Nicaragua, the largest freshwater lake in Central America. It's also home to the world's only freshwater sharks. It, too, has been extremely polluted by industrial waste and sewage. To date, no water treatment facilities have been built to help fix either lake's environmental problems.

Nicaraguan Wildlife

The endangered sea turtle is the country's best-known creature. Thousands of them make an annual journey to the beach to lay their eggs and return to the sea. Unfortunately, only a few of the newly hatched turtles live because predators like the seagull get to them. About 35,000 adult turtles are killed illegally each year for their eggs and meat. Extensive efforts are being made to preserve them, including a sea turtle nursery on the Pacific Coast.

Sea turtle

Nicaragua is known throughout the world for its big cats. These include the stealthy jaguar (the largest of the cats), the cougar, the smaller ocelot, and the spotted margay of the rainforest. A few of the more unusual animals in Nicaragua include the armadillo, the anteater, and the three-toed sloth.

In Nicaragua you'll find butterflies, moths, beetles, mosquitoes, grasshoppers, dragonflies, and the praying mantis. But one of the most unusual insects is the walking stick. They're tough to spot in the wild because they're so well camouflaged.

Marine life includes whales, dolphins, sharks, stingrays, barracudas, and thousands of tropical fish. Besides the sea life, the water holds spectacular colorful reefs and lots of ocean flora. It's no wonder that diving and snorkeling are popular here.

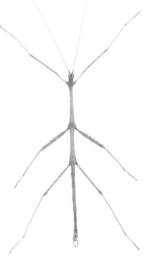

Walking stick

Find the Secret Bird

Birds, birds, birds! They're all over Nicaragua. You'll find them in the city, in the country, on the shores, and gliding along the seas. Unscramble the names of these birds found in Nicaragua. Use the list to help you. Then write each boxed letter in the spaces at the bottom of the page. What's the secret bird?

ALTAMIRA ORIOLE	ROYAL TERN
BLACK HAWK EAGLE	SNAIL KITE
GREY GULL	SNOWY EGRET
KISKADEE	SPECTACLED OWL
LIMPKIN	TROPICAL KINGBIRD
MUSCOVY DUCK	WHITE WINGED DOVE

1. VYOCSUM   DKUC   _ _ _ _ _ _ _ _ _

2. CLDEEPSCTA   LOW   _ _ _ _ _ _ _ _ _ _ _ _

3. EEDAKKIS   _ _ _ _ _ _ _

4. CALPORTI   GBIRDKIN   _ _ _ _ _ _ _ _ _ _ _ _ _ _ _ _

5. EYRG   LLUG   _ _ _ _ _ _ _ _

6. LAYOR   NRET   _ _ _ _ _ _ _ _ _

7. WYSON   RETGE   _ _ _ _ _ _ _ _ _ _ _

8. LMIPNIK   _ _ _ _ _ _ _

9. AALTARIM   IORLEO   _ _ _ _ _ _ _ _ _ _ _ _ _

10. CLABK   KHAW   LEAGE   _ _ _ _ _ _ _ _ _ _ _ _ _ _

11. ILANS   ETIK   _ _ _ _ _ _ _ _ _

12. HITEW   EDGNIW   OVED   _ _ _ _ _ _ _ _ _ _ _ _ _ _ _

THE SECRET BIRD IS THE ___ __ __ __ __ __ __   __ __ __ __ __ __

Pre-Columbian People

Nicaragua is named for Chief Nicara, leader of the indigenous people that lived around Lake Nicaragua in the late 1400s and early 1500s. We know little about the people who lived in the country prior to the 1400s. However, there is evidence of some early villages south of Bluefields in the Caribbean Lowlands that may date back about 8,000 years. At an archaeological site in Managua is a set of footprints preserved in the volcanic mud that dates back about 6,000 years.

Unfortunately, much of Nicaragua's history before the arrival of the Spanish in the 16th century has been lost. We do know that an Aztec calendar and images of their god Quetzalcóatl found in Nicaragua date back to about 800 CE. A number of groups lived on the Atlantic Coast, including the Mayanga and the Miskito people. We still just don't know where they came from!

Arrival of the Spanish and British

Christopher Columbus was the first European known to have reached Nicaragua as he sailed south along the Central American isthmus in 1502. On his fourth voyage, Columbus explored the Mosquito Coast along the Caribbean Lowlands in the east.

Córdoba

The conquistador Francisco Hernández de Córdoba founded the first permanent Spanish settlements on the country's Pacific coast in 1524. These included Granada on Lake Nicaragua and León east of Lake Managua. The first European settlement was founded on the Atlantic Coast by the British Providence Company.

Although rival companies of conquistadors clashed in their efforts to rule the country, they succeeded in killing or enslaving most of the natives. The natives' land was then parceled out to the conquistadors. Many native people were enslaved and forced to develop these estates—many of which were in western Nicaragua. Others worked the mines in the north, and still others were sent to New World Spanish colonies. Finally, many died from disease and neglect.

Independence from Spain

Nicaragua gained its independence from Spain in 1821. It was briefly a part of the Mexican Empire and a member country of the federation of independent Central American provinces. However, it became an independent republic in 1838.

Civil war exploded in 1855 between the wealthy Liberals of León and the wealthy Conservatives of Granada. The Liberals invited an American from Tennessee, William Walker, and his 300 professional soldiers to fight against the Conservatives. In a surprise move, Walker seized the Presidency of Nicaragua in 1856. He wanted to make Nicaragua a slave state of the United States. In the historic Battle of San Jacinto, now celebrated on September 14 as a national holiday, his troops fought both the Liberals and the Conservatives. They joined forces to drive Walker out of office in 1857.

In 1858, Managua replaced León as the country's capital. (Managua is still the capital today). This was an attempt to reduce the rivalry between the liberal León and conservative Granada.

Thirty years of peaceful Conservative rule followed. Nicaragua developed a close relationship with the United States. But a Liberal named Jose Santos Zelaya led a revolt that brought him to power in 1893. Great Britain had been occupying the Caribbean Coast of Nicaragua since the first half of the 19th century. Under Zalaya's leadership, the British gave the Caribbean coast back to Nicaragua.

In the 1800s, waves of immigrants—particularly from Germany, Italy, Spain, France, and Belgium—moved to Nicaragua. They set up many farming businesses, like coffee and sugarcane plantations.

The Twentieth Century

Zelaya rejected a U.S. proposal to build a canal through Nicaragua to link the Pacific and Atlantic Oceans. The United States turned to Panama and began construction of the famous Panama Canal in 1904. Zelaya was unsuccessful in his attempts to interest Germany and Japan in building a similar canal. His political strength was weakening with the wealthy upper classes. To protect Americans living in Nicaragua, the United States provided military support to Conservative forces in 1909 that were rebelling against Zelaya.

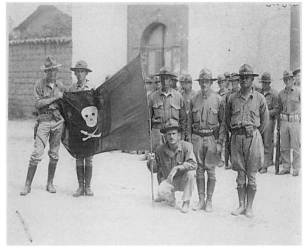

U.S. Marines capture flag of Sandino, 1932

For the next 20 years, the United States dominated Nicaraguan politics. In 1914 the Bryan-Chamorro Treaty granted the United States the exclusive right to build a canal in Nicaragua. America really had no intention of building a canal; it simply wanted to stop anyone else from building one! American troops remained in Nicaragua from 1912 to 1933. From 1927 to 1933, U.S. Marines in Nicaragua constantly battled rebel forces led by Liberal General Augusto Sandino.

The United States only pulled out of Nicaragua when pressure in the country along with the demands of the Great Depression in America forced out the U.S. troops. After they left the country, National Guard Commander Anastasio Somoza Garcia took over the presidency of Nicaragua in 1936. Sandino was assassinated by National Guard officers. Somoza and his two sons who ruled as dictators after him maintained close ties with the United States—particularly the Kennedy administration.

The Sandinista Regime

The Somoza dynasty ended in 1979 with a massive civil war led by the Sandinista National Liberation Front (FSLN). This group of radical university students had been fighting the Somoza regime since the early 1960s. When the Sandinistas came to power in 1979, Daniel Ortega became a member of the ruling military government and later served as Nicaraguan president twice—from 1985 to 1990 and from 2006 to the present.

But the Sandinistas took over a broken country filled with poverty, homelessness, and other social problems. In addition, about 50,000 people had been killed in the ongoing revolution.

The FSLN established a strong dictatorship, and ties with the United States fell apart. The regime took over private industries, private farms, and private property. It also forged ties to many international terrorist movements in Latin America and elsewhere. The Nicaraguan Constitution was suspended. The Congress was dissolved. The Sandinista People's Army replaced the National Guard.

The United States stopped sending aid to Nicaragua in 1981. Throughout much of the 1980s, President Ronald Reagan's administration provided aid to the resistance groups like the Contras who were opposing the Sandinistas. In 1985, the United States stopped all trade with Nicaragua.

The Sandinista regime agreed to negotiate with the Nicaraguan resistance and hold nationwide elections in February 1990. International observers declared these elections free and fair. Violeta Barrios de Chamorro, the National Opposition Union Candidate, defeated Daniel Ortega and became the new Nicaraguan President. The United States finally lifted its trade embargo. But by this time, the country was in economic ruin.

Free Elections and Democracy

President Chamorro's seven-year government helped bring progress and democracy to Nicaragua. She had the backing of the United States. The economy stabilized, state-owned businesses were given back to private owners, and human rights abuses were greatly reduced.

Free elections were once again held in 1996. Former Managua Mayor Arnoldo Alemán, leader of the Liberal Alliance, was elected president. The first transfer of power from one democratically-elected president to another took place on January 10, 1997. Unfortunately, the Alemán administration was very corrupt. He pulled about $100 million out of the government's treasury for his own use. Daniel Ortega once again surfaced in Nicaraguan politics. At the end of his term, Alemán and Ortega made a pact to divide control of the state organizations of power between them.

In the midst of this political upheaval, Hurricane Mitch devastated Nicaragua in 1998. The second deadliest hurricane in history, it dropped record amounts of rain on the country, causing a mudslide that was ten miles long and five miles wide. Two million people were affected, and more than 500,000 were driven from their homes. The total damage was $1 billion. The country is still recovering.

In 2001 Enrique Bolaños of the Liberal Constitutional Party was elected president, defeating FSLN candidate Daniel Ortega by a small margin. Bolaños had anything but a smooth presidency. Although he promised to create jobs, boost the economy, and fight terrorism and corruption, both Liberals and Conservatives repeatedly attacked his administration.

The Sandinistas: Once Again

FSLN candidate Daniel Ortega once again won the presidency in 2006. International observers, however, were not allowed to witness this election as they had been since 1990. There were reports made of violence against those who opposed Ortega. There were claims that completed ballots were destroyed and that vote tallies were altered. As a result of these claims, the United States stopped $64 million in U.S. aid to Nicaragua. The European Union suspended $70 million. Despite all of these claims, Daniel Ortega was inaugurated president, once again, in 2007. His term will last five years.

Nicaragua Today

Nicaragua remains the second-poorest nation in the Western Hemisphere. It is still rebuilding from the devastating effects of Hurricane Mitch. Crime has increased drastically as more people slip into poverty. Daniel Ortega has suggested that he wants to change the Constitution so he'll be allowed to run for President again after his current term is up. The Nicaraguan economy remains extremely weak. International tourists are beginning to discover Nicaragua's incredible beauty, but this is only the beginning of a long road to prosperity and democracy.

Daily Life

Personal pride—no matter a person's education, age, or income level—is very important in Nicaragua. National pride is important, too. Perhaps more than any other Central or South American country, Nicaraguans have extreme pride in their country.

The Family Unit

Nuclear and Extended Family
The family unit is the focus of Nicaraguan life. The nuclear family includes the mother, father, brothers, and sisters. The extended family members that include grandparents, cousins, aunts, and uncles are equally important and provide lifelong support. Newly married couples may move in with the bride's or the groom's parents until they can afford their own home.

Godparents
A child's godmother (*madrina*) and godfather (*padrino*) help the child achieve a better life through the *compadrazgo* system. This is the relationship between the child, the parents, and the godparents.

Godparents are usually trusted friends of the parents. They are expected to be very concerned about the child's well-being, and may even help the child achieve a higher social status. Thus, lower-class families might choose wealthy godparents, or wealthy people may choose godchildren who will become part of their support network. A wealthy businesswoman, for example, may give a job to her godchild.

Family Size
Six, eight, or even more family members often live under one roof. It's common for extended family members to live with the nuclear family. Everyone in the household does daily chores. Children may start working when they are little, selling fruit and vegetables on the streets or in the markets. Some kids may even work before they go to school each day.

Nicaraguan Homes and Buildings

Nicaraguan Homes
The average home for a person who lives above the poverty level is made of cement or wood and has a metal roof. Sometimes the floor is tiled; sometimes it's simply dirt. The homes are very open due to the hot weather, so it's common to see mice, geckoes, and other crawling creatures in the homes. Some homes have a kitchen, and some only have a wood-burning stove.

The more substantial homes of the middle and upper classes are usually built in the Spanish or Mediterranean style. But even these will not be over-decorated or overfilled with furniture. People are very aware that earthquakes can ruin their possessions *and* their homes in a few short minutes.

Shelter for the Poor
Some 75 percent of Nicaraguans all over the country live in extreme poverty, often in crowded settlements on the outskirts of major cities. The poorest live in rickety, open shelters that provide no protection or privacy. Often it is abandoned kids who live in these makeshift homes and pick through garbage dumps for food. Many international humanitarian and religious groups go to Nicaragua each year to help educate these kids and provide them with food, clothing, and shelter.

The poorest people in the rural areas live in palm-front huts supported by poles. The floor is dirt, and there is very little room. There is usually no running water or electricity in the house. All in all, the conditions are very primitive.

Rebuilding Cities and Preserving the Past

The business district of Managua was totally destroyed in the 1972 earthquake. Rebuilding this area is an ongoing process, and there are now many new high-rise commercial and apartment buildings. Plans are underway to build a monorail system and to reconstruct the old center of Managua. There is still a housing shortage in the city, but there are now extensive suburbs stretching out from it.

National Palace in Managua

Some of Nicaragua's most beautiful Spanish colonial homes and churches are found in the major cities like Managua, León, and Granada. Their narrow streets, red-tiled roofs, and substantial buildings radiate old-world charm. Granada, which is now a major tourist destination, has some of the best-preserved colonial architecture in the country.

Going to School

Education in Nicaragua is free. Kids between the ages of six and 13 must go to school. Classes in most parts of the country are taught in Spanish. Students on the Caribbean coast have classes in their native languages. After school, kids participate in organized activities, like learning Nicaraguan folk dances.

Granada

Unfortunately, many Nicaraguan kids still don't get an education—particularly those in the rural areas where there are no schools. Bringing the educational system of Nicaragua up to the standards of other school systems in Latin America has been a long, hard struggle. In 1979, the Nicaraguan school system was the poorest in Latin America. When the Sandinista government took over in 1980, it created a successful literacy campaign to get more kids reading and writing. High school students, university students, and teachers volunteered to tutor and significantly improved Nicaraguan children's literacy rate. The struggle to educate more kids continues, but the situation has vastly improved since 1979.

For those who want to go on to higher education, most of the universities, colleges, and technical institutes are in Managua. The technical schools offer courses of study in electronics, computers, forestry, construction, and other trade-related services.

Are We There Yet?

Most people in Nicaragua travel by bus within and between the larger cities because it's the cheapest way to go. Many of the buses are old yellow U.S. school buses called "Chicken Buses" that have been repainted and redecorated. Managua has many bus lines. Each one is individually owned and has its own fares and routes. The buses are extremely crowded and sometimes unsafe because pickpockets take advantage of the crowding to steal purses and wallets.

For those who want to travel cross-country, there's always the microbus. These minibuses are like airport vans and hold up to 15 people. They run regular routes between Managua and nearby cities like Granada and León.

Taxis are a great way to get around Managua, and there are lots of them. But tourists tend to take taxis more than locals do. Many people often share one cab. Unlike North American cabs, Nicaraguan cabs do not have meters. The driver and the customers agree on the fare before the trip begin.

Driving a personal car is difficult and sometimes risky. It's okay if you use the four main freeways that run through Managua. They're in good condition—even though bicycles, oxcarts, dogs, and horses sometimes pose a traffic hazard! But most roads outside the major cities are unpaved, and seasonal rains take a heavy toll on them. Although there are posted speed limits, traffic rules often are not enforced.

Famous Nicaraguans

Rubén Darío (1867–1916) was a Nicaraguan poet, diplomat, and national hero. He became known for his poetry when he was just 12 years old. He is best known for starting the literary movement known as *modernism*.

Bianca Jagger (1945–) is best known for being married to Mick Jagger of the Rolling Stones. However, she works and travels extensively for humanitarian causes, particularly in Latin America.

Gioconda Belli (1948–) is a world-renowned poet. She has been named one of the 100 most important poets of the 20th century.

Christianne Meneses Jacobs (1971) is publisher of *Iguana*, the only Spanish-language magazine for kids in North America.

Body Language and Etiquette in Nicaragua
Here are some examples of body language and etiquette you'll find in Nicaragua.

Even in the warm climate, businessmen wear business suits with ties, long-sleeved shirts, and trousers. Businesswomen wear business dresses or suits.

Men greet men with a handshake. Women greet women with a handshake. Family and friends greet each other with a light hug and a kiss on the cheek.

It's common for Nicaraguans to drop in on each other without arranging to get together.

Nicaraguans are extremely polite and avoid saying anything offensive.

It's common for Nicaraguans to stare at foreigners, particularly in rural areas.

Showing up 30 to 60 minutes late for an event or meeting is acceptable.

People point with their lips. They pucker their lips and raise their chin in the direction of the person or thing to which they're pointing.

A taxi driver or bus driver who wags his finger at a person on the street is asking if the person wants a ride.

Rubbing the index fingers together means the person wants to pay for something.

Crinkling the nose means, "I don't understand what you mean!"

Know Before You Go

Nicaraguans called themselves *Nicas*. If you go to the Atlantic Coast, people are likely to speak English in addition to Spanish. On the Pacific side of the country, they'll speak Spanish. Check out page 15 for some common phrases you will use in Nicaragua.

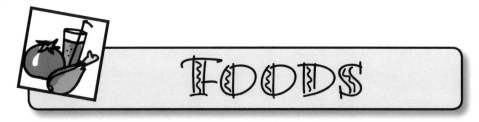

FOODS

Nicaraguan Cuisine: The Staples

Corn

Nicaraguans call themselves "sons of corn." Since pre-Columbian times, corn has been at the center of the Nicaraguan diet. It is used in main dishes, desserts, and even in drinks. Here are a few favorites.

- A *nacatamal* is a corn tamale much bigger than the tamales in Mexico. Each nacatamal is a meal in itself, with corn, rice, meat, and other ingredients wrapped in a banana or plantain leaf. They're eaten at Christmas and on special occasions, or during a weekly lunch or dinner.

- *Indio viejo* is a dish made with long strings of meat or chicken mixed with corn meal.

- *Sopa de albóndigas* is meatball soup—corn meal gives the meatballs flavor and texture and holds them together.

- *Atole* is a delicious cornstarch-based hot drink that includes cinnamon, vanilla, and chocolate. The version with chocolate is a popular snack at Christmas with tamales.

- *Pinolillo,* the national drink of Nicaragua, is a sweet cornmeal and cocoa drink that has a gritty texture. Nicaraguans even call themselves *Pinoleros.*

Pinolillo gourds

Fruits

Some of the common fruits grown and eaten in Nicaragua have probably never crossed your dining table! Here are just a few that might be new to you.

- *Jocote* is a flowering plant that produces a fruit with a large seed. They are eaten ripe with no seasoning, or unripe with salt. Street vendors sell bags of them.

- Ripe *mangoes* have a sweet taste and a pulpy flesh. Although they originated in India, they're now a very popular fruit in Central America. In Nicaragua they're eaten ripe or green with salt, pepper, and hot sauce. Street vendors sell lots of these, too!

- *Tamarind* fruit grows in long, brown pods on a large, tropical tree. The pods contain seeds in a juicy pulp. In Central America, tamarind is dried, salted, candied, used in desserts, made into jam, blended into drinks, or put in ice cream. Sometimes the seeds and juicy pulp are combined with water and processed to create a juice with a strong taste. There are large tamarind plantations in Nicaragua.

Tamarind

- A *plantain* is a starchy relative of a banana. It's not sweet enough or soft enough to be eaten raw, so it's often cut in half or cut in round "disks" and fried twice. Then the pieces are removed from the oil, pounded flat, and fried again. Nicaraguans also eat them sliced very thinly, fried, and cooled, like potato chips.

- *Breadfruit* is a big, oval-shaped fruit that grows on a large tree, and it really does taste like bread. It has a thick rind, like pineapple, that cannot be eaten. The white inner flesh has no seeds. It's cooked, fried, or baked, and it really can end up looking like a slice of bread!

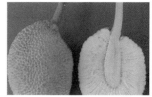
Breadfruit

Beans and Rice
Most people eat *gallo pinto* (spotted rooster), a blend of precooked rice and beans, several times a week. Like pinolillo, it's a national dish of Nicaragua.

Yucca
Yucca (also called cassava or manioc) is a woody shrub that has a starchy, tuberous root. Nicaraguans love it with pork rind and beans. It can be boiled and eaten as a potato substitute or made into soups, stews, and gravies. It is made into flour, cereals, cakes, and puddings, and people sell it at roadside stands.

Meats
Nicaraguans waste little when preparing meat dishes. A Nicaraguan dish may include the tail, the brain, and the stomach. If preparing a pork dish, the skin, blood, and ears may be used. *Chicharrón,* for example, is a dish made of fried pork rinds—pork skin that has been seasoned and deep fried. This is one of Nicaragua's most popular snacks.

Daily Meals

Nicaraguans may eat two to three meals a day, depending on how much a family can afford. Since about 75 percent of the people live in poverty, two meals a day would be about normal. People generally eat their main meal at midday and take a *siesta* (afternoon nap) afterward.

For everyone, no matter how much money they have, each meal is likely to include corn tortillas. Nicaraguan tortillas are large and made of white corn. They're eaten plain or used as a "wrapper" for other foods served at the meal, like meat and beans.

Beans and rice are served daily. The popular gallo pinto is usually a breakfast dish. Other variations of beans and rice will appear at lunch and dinner, too. Foods eaten regularly are eggs, meat, simple salads (cabbages and tomatoes), and fruit. Special celebration meals are likely to include grilled steak (for those who can afford it).

Coffee is a favorite drink. At breakfast people drink it with hot milk, and the rest of the day they drink it black with sugar.

Holidays & Festivals

Holy Week and Easter
(Date Varies)

For Christians, the Easter season celebrates the resurrection of Jesus. In Nicaragua, this important Christian holiday is also the summer vacation period. So, many people are free to take part in religious processions, rituals, and services. Those who don't participate in the religious tradition spend a lot of time at the beach. The tropical temperatures soar during this time of year. Towns along both Nicaraguan coasts are often packed with vacationers.

Nicaraguan beach

Palm Sunday

In the Christian tradition, Holy Week consists of the six days (from Palm Sunday to Holy Saturday) that lead up to Easter Sunday. In Nicaragua, thousands of people take part in various Holy Week processions that start with a donkey procession on Palm Sunday. This recreates the entry of Jesus into Jerusalem on a donkey, when massive crowds greeted him with palms. A statue of Jesus is set on a live donkey. The faithful walk with the donkey in a procession that lasts several hours.

Stations of the Cross

The Stations of the Cross is the story about Jesus' painful journey to his death. This is represented by 14 stops he is supposed to have made along the way. Stations of the Cross processions take place every Friday during Lent (the 40-day period before Easter). People walk a statue of Jesus through the street, stopping 14 times at houses where altars are set up. The final Stations of the Cross procession is on Good Friday.

Good Friday

The Service of Darkness on Good Friday is the most solemn day of the Christian church year. It symbolizes Christ's death and burial. A somber procession begins at each church where Christ's statue is placed in a casket. It is carried around the streets; people in the procession hold candles and torches.

Easter

The Easter procession is joyous and filled with music. In cities and towns all over Nicaragua, people from one church start a procession carrying a statue of Jesus. People from another church start a procession carrying a statue of Mary. The two processions meet, which symbolizes Jesus reuniting with Mary after his resurrection. The reunion is met with shouts of happiness by the crowd.

One Easter Tradition that Goes to the Dogs!

Many places in Nicaragua have different traditions to celebrate the Easter season. One of the most fun and famous is held in Masaya Province, close to Managua. On a Sunday morning a few weeks before Holy Week, hundreds of people bring their dogs to the Santa María Magdalena Church for the procession of San Lázaro, the patron saint of pets.

But these aren't just *any* dogs—they're dogs in costume! Inside the church, benches are removed and the floor is covered with sand to make it easier to clean up after hundreds of dogs. A special service is held, and awards are given to the best-dressed pooches.

Hundreds of people from all over the country join in the fun. They give thanks for special favors and offer prayers for special needs.

Revolution Day
July 19
This holiday marks the defeat of the 40-year Somoza dictatorship dynasty in 1979 by the Sandinista National Liberation Front. It celebrates the Sandinistas coming to power and is marked by cultural presentations and festivals.

Festival of Santo Domingo de Guzmán (Managua)
August 1–10
Each city in Nicaragua has its own patron saint and annual festival to celebrate his or her life. Managua's Festival of Saint Domingo is the most famous of the country's festivals.

Holy Domingo de Guzmán was a missionary and a protector of Nicaragua's slaves who lived from 1170 to 1221. He is the patron saint of Managua, and his life is celebrated every year with a huge festival held August 1 to August 10.

The festival features lots of events, and thousands of people fill the streets. A statue of Saint Domingo is carried through the city on August 1 from Las Sierritas church in south Managua to another church in the north. The statue remains there until August 10 when it is returned to Las Sierritas.

Every day from the opening to the closing of the festival is one giant street party that draws people from all over the world. The festival begins with a long parade. People dress up in costumes and masks, local businesses decorate their cars and trucks, and horse riders from Nicaragua and other Central American countries show off their horses, costumes, and riding skills.

San Jacinto Day and Independence Day
September 14 and September 15
On September 14, Nicaraguans commemorate the 1856 Battle of San Jacinto in which William Walker and his men were defeated. Walker, an American, had seized the Presidency of Nicaragua in 1856 and tried to make the country a slave state of the United States.

On September 15, people from Nicaragua, Guatemala, Honduras, El Salvador, and Costa Rica—no matter where they happen to be in the world—all celebrate Central America's declaration of independence in 1821.

One of the most important elements of both holidays is flying the Nicaraguan flag from homes and businesses throughout the country. Traditional dances, music, costumes, and cultural events round out the party agenda. Keeping traditions alive and handing them down to the next generation are at the heart of both of these holidays, especially Independence Day. Above all, love of country is celebrated!

Dia de los Muertos (Day of the Dead)
November 2
Day of the Dead is a special holiday to honor relatives and friends who have died. Actually, it's more like a day to celebrate life. The real message of Day of the Dead is, "Death does not separate us!"

All over Nicaragua, flower stalls fills the streets. People buy bunches of flowers and create beautiful arrangements. Then they go to the cemeteries and clean up the gravesites of loved ones. This may include pulling weeds, putting in new plants, and even repainting the gravestones. They then place a special bouquet of flowers on each grave.

Dia de los Muertos

The Christmas Season

December is a month of celebration in Nicaragua. It's filled with get-togethers, special foods, parties, processions, and fireworks. In the weeks before Christmas, many families and businesses put up a Christmas tree decorated with lights, bells, and ornaments. The other and perhaps even more important symbol set up in homes and churches is a nativity scene (called *El Nacimiento*). Some people do not put the image of the Jesus into the scene until the early morning hours of December 25.

Immaculate Conception Day (La Purisma, December 8)

Nicaraguans love this special holiday that honors the Virgin Mary. It's one of the happiest celebrations of the year. It starts on the evening of December 7 (called *La Gritera*) when people set off fireworks and celebrate for hours.

Most people have a richly decorated altar in their home with a statue of the Virgin Mary on it. For many families, the statue itself has been passed down through several generations. On December 8, family members, friends, and neighbors gather in front of the altar to pray, sing, eat traditional foods and sweets, and open gifts. Afterward, everyone in the neighborhood sets off firecrackers—again!

Christmas (December 24 and 25)

Midnight on December 24 is the magic hour for celebrating Nicaraguan Christmas. Families send their kids to bed and wake them up at midnight to see the gifts that Santa brought them. Also at midnight, everyone sets off fireworks. Family members, friends, and neighbors hug each other as a sign of love and forgiveness. The official Christmas dinner is served at midnight.

New Year's (December 31)

A long-standing tradition in Nicaragua is to symbolically burn away the old year. Some people do this by dressing a doll in old clothes and hanging it up in the streets. When the New Year comes, they burn the doll and, along with it, burn the bad things from the old year. After this ritual, they set off fireworks and have a special dinner at midnight followed by the first party of the New Year.

The Epiphany (Three Kings Day, January 6)

Also called Three Kings Day, this holiday honors the Three Wise Men who brought gifts to the baby Jesus. Like in other Latin American countries, Nicaraguan kids get gifts on this day. The holiday often ends with a fireworks display.

Creative Arts

Music and Dance

For centuries Nicaraguans have expressed the happy and sad events of their lives through music and dance. Traditional dance groups exist all over the country. To watch a dance is to watch a story. Some dances feature masked characters. For example, one traditional dance theme is reenacting the Spanish conquest. The Spanish conquerors are depicted by dancers wearing pink masks with ugly features and expressions.

Voladores

In one fantastic dance called the *palo volador,* the dancer is strapped to a rope wound around a high pole. The dancer then unwinds, swinging farther away from the pole to the pounding of percussion instruments like drums. This reenacts the descent of the angels to battle the forces of darkness in the underworld.

On the Caribbean coast, *palo de mayo* (maypole) is a key traditional form of dance and music. It's commonly performed during the month-long May Day Festival in Bluefields. Celebrating the first of May (May Day) is one of the highlights of the year in Caribbean Nicaragua. Performers dance around a maypole decorated with colored ribbons in celebration of the arrival of spring and new life.

Nicaraguan music mixes the tone and rhythm of the native Nicaraguan people with the Spanish who settled the country. The *marimba*—which is similar to the xylophone—gives Nicaraguan music its distinct sound. The marimba is a common instrument in all Central America countries. In Nicaragua, the musician holds the instrument on his or her knees and is usually accompanied by a bass fiddle, guitar, and a *guitarrilla* (a small guitar).

Marimba

Reggae music is popular all over Nicaragua. Developed in Jamaica in the 1960s, reggae can get anybody moving! It has a very simple beat and repetitive chords. Once you hear it, you have to dance to it!

Daily Dress

It's hot in Nicaragua much of the year, and the everyday clothing reflects the temperature. Women usually wear a simple cotton dress. Men wear work shirts, jeans, sneakers or sandals, and straw hats. Men may also wear the *guayabera* (also called the Havana shirt or the Mexican wedding shirt). It's a light cotton shirt with beautiful embroidery on it.

Traditional dress for women varies in each region of the country. In the western city of Masaya, which is called the heart of Nicaraguan folklore, women wear a long cotton skirt and a colorful short-sleeved cotton blouse, both of which are embroidered. A shawl, a necklace, earrings, and a flower in the hair complete the outfit. Women usually don't wear shoes or sandals. Men wear blue cotton trousers, a long-sleeved collarless white cotton shirt, a machete (a large knife) in a sheath that is strapped to the waist, a straw hat, and sandals.

Folklore

Nicaraguan folklore is filled with tall tales, fables, and popular "trickster" characters like *Pedro Urdemales* and *Uncle Rabbit* who use their wits to fool the powerful.

You'll see some of the most vivid and interesting costumes in Nicaragua's folk performances like *El Güegüense* (The Old Man). This is one of the oldest theatrical works in the Western Hemisphere and combines music, dance, and theater. It was written in the 16th century and has been handed down through many generations.

Folk practices are alive and well in Nicaragua. Most households display a picture of a saint to help protect the home and answer prayers. Celebrations of the feast days of city, town, or village patron saints are held during planting and harvest in the belief that the saint's blessing will help produce good crops. Healers will use many native crops and plants to produce medicines.

Poetry

José Coronel Urtecho, a great Nicaraguan poet, once said, "Every Nicaraguan is a poet until proven otherwise." Poetry is more important in Nicaragua than anywhere else in Latin America. The first Latin American nominated for a Nobel Prize for Literature was Salomón de la Selva, a Nicaraguan poet. Nicaraguans begin learning poetry when they are very young. Even first graders will memorize the poetry of Rubén Darío (1867–1916), the country's much-loved national hero. Darío is so loved in Nicaragua that his portrait is on the country's 100 cordoba note.

Ruben Darío

Nicaraguan newspapers and popular magazines publish poetry. The subjects can includes anything from love to criticizing the government. In Nicaragua, the word *poet* has such a positive meaning that people even use it in place of the word *friend* or *buddy*.

Each year, the city of Granada hosts an International Poetry Festival. Poets from all over the world recite their work to admiring crowds. The beautiful colonial buildings, plazas, churches, and market areas are all great places for poetry readings. There are also concerts, carnivals, music, and dance.

Folk Art

For almost 30 years, Nicaragua's Ministry of Culture has been preserving folk art by training artists to make traditional handicrafts. Today the country's fine folk art includes hammocks, baskets, embroidered blouses, wood carvings, leather work, coral jewelry, painted gourds, and dolls. The city of Masaya is called the "Cradle of Nicaraguan Folklore." At the Masaya's Artisans Market you'll find stall after stall of these unique items.

Masaya mask

Make a Miniature Maypole

The tradition of making and dancing around a maypole on May 1 (May Day) is centuries old. A maypole is a tall, wooden pole with lots of long, brightly-colored ribbons suspended from the top of it. It can also be decorated with lots of flowers, greens, and wreaths. In many parts of the world, like Nicaragua, people dance around the maypole, holding on to the ribbons and weaving them in and out. It's a fun way to welcome spring! Follow the directions below to make your own miniature maypole.

Materials

- paper towel cardboard roll
- stiff piece of cardboard
- several colors of ribbon that are ¼ in. to ½ in. wide
- tape or glue
- scissors
- tempera paints
- brushes
- water bowl, water, and cloth for cleaning paint brushes
- optional: glitter, artificial greens, artificial flowers

Directions

1. Paint the paper towel maypole roll a bright color.

2. Paint the stiff piece of cardboard the same color as the maypole roll.

3. Allow the maypole and the cardboard stand to dry thoroughly.

4. Either tape or glue one end of the maypole to the cardboard stand.

5. Tape a ribbon to the top of the maypole. Wrap the ribbon around the pole, on a diagonal, until you reach the bottom. The ribbon should look like it alternates with the color of the maypole. Tape the ribbon to the bottom of the maypole.

6. Cut several lengths of ribbon long enough to reach from the top of the maypole to the bottom of it.

7. Tape the ribbons to the inside edge at the top of the maypole. They should hang down outside the maypole.

8. Further decorate your maypole with glitter, artificial greens, or artificial

Sports & Games

Baseball

Baseball is the most popular sport in Nicaragua. It came to the country in the late 19th century and caught on quickly. Five teams in Nicaragua compete with each other. The best players from these teams make up the national team when Nicaragua competes internationally. The Nicaraguan national team is considered the best in Central America, alongside Panama's team. It finished fourth at the 1996 Summer Olympics and most recently took a bronze medal in the 2007 Pan American games.

Nicaragua has had its share of star players who made it to Major League Baseball (MLB) in America. Dennis Martínez (1955–) was the first. He was the first Latin-born pitcher to throw a perfect game when he played with the Montreal Expos in 1991. He's so well-respected that he was called *El Presidente* (The President) during his career. Nicaragua's national stadium in Managua was renamed Dennis Martínez National Stadium in 1998.

Two other famous Nicaraguan players also made it to MLB. Vicente Padilla (1977–) has pitched for many teams, including the Los Angeles Dodgers. Devern Hansack (1978–) last pitched for the Boston Red Sox.

Boxing

After baseball, Nicaraguans love boxing. World champion Alexis Argüello (1952–2009), called "The Explosive Thin Man," was a three-time world champion boxer. After his retirement from boxing, he went into politics. He was mayor of Managua from 2008 until his death in 2009. Ricardo Mayorga (1973–) has been called the craziest man in the sport of boxing because of his fearless fighting style. His nickname is *El Matador* (The Bullfighter).

Surf's Up

As Nicaragua becomes more visible to the world, it's becoming more of a destination for surfers. Most beaches aren't crowded, so there's a lot of room. Lake Nicaragua in the south-central part of the country covers a huge surface of some 5,000 square miles and has almost constant offshore wind, which creates great waves. It also helps to create an ideal feeding ground for fish. Surfers can ride the waves and observe the abundant marine life like dolphins, whales, turtles, and schools of tropical fish. Popoyo Beach in the Rivas area of southwestern Nicaragua is the most famous place to surf in the country.

Panama

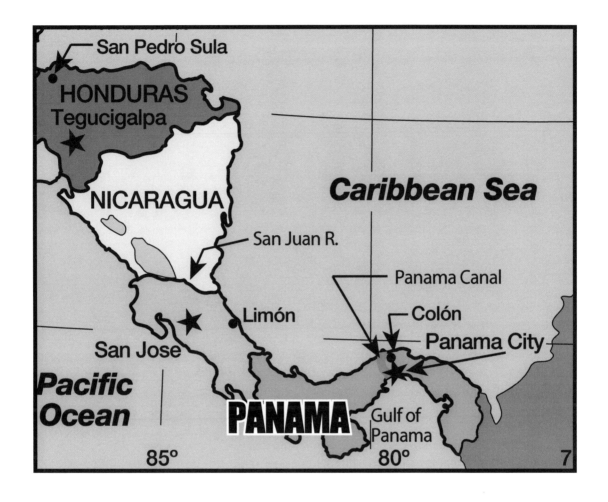

San Pedro Sula

HONDURAS
Tegucigalpa

NICARAGUA

Caribbean Sea

San Juan R.

Panama Canal

Colón

Panama City

Limón

San Jose

Pacific Ocean

PANAMA

Gulf of Panama

85°

80°

7

Welcome to Panama!

Panama has always been a country at a crossroads. It is on the Isthmus of Panama, a narrow strip of land that connects North and South America. For such a small country in area, Panama has played a big part in the world's economy with the building and now the expansion of the Panama Canal. But Panama is more than a country with a waterway. Its unique location as a land bridge allowed prehistoric people to inhabit South America. It is Panama's location—with its beautiful coasts, thick forests, and lively capital city—that still draws people to it today.

After you have finished learning about Panama, be sure to check out page 148 for additional classroom activities.

FAST FACTS

Official Name:	Republic of Panama
Location:	Central America. Panama is bordered by the Caribbean Sea on the north, Colombia on the east, North Pacific Ocean on the south, and Costa Rica on the west.
Population:	3,360,474 (2010 estimate)
Capital City:	Panama City
Area:	29,159 square miles. Panama is slightly smaller than the state of South Carolina.
Major Languages:	Spanish (official) English (14%) Many Panamanians are bilingual.
Major Religion:	Christianity (predominantly Roman Catholic)
Currency:	The U.S. dollar (the legal currency) 1 dollar = 100 cents The balboa (the Panamanian currency) 1 balboa = 100 centésimos
Climate:	Tropical with little seasonal variation The rainy season is from mid-April through December. The dry season is from January through early April.
The Land:	A central spine of mountains and hills with peaks formed by volcanoes. Swamps occur along both coasts; forests and grasslands dominate the lowland interior. There are jungles in the northeast.
Type of Government:	Constitutional democracy

Flag:

The Panamanian flag is divided into four equal rectangles. The top quadrants are white (on the hoist side) with a blue five-pointed star in the center, and plain red. The bottom quadrants are plain blue (on the hoist side) and white with a red five-pointed star in the center. The flag was adopted in 1949 and reflects the political situation at the time. The stars and rectangles stand for the two main political parties. Blue was the color of the Conservatives, and red was the color of the Liberals. White represents their peaceful cooperation.

Coat of Arms:

Panama's coat of arms is complex and reflects its history. The center section shows the Isthmus of Panama. The top part of the coat of arms is divided into two quarters. In the top left quarter are a crossed sword and rifle on a silver field; they symbolize abandonment of civil wars. In the top right quarter are a crossed shovel and hoe on a red background; they symbolize work.

The bottom part of the coat of arms is also divided into two quarters. In the lower left quarter is a cornucopia on a blue field; it symbolizes wealth. In the lower right quarter is a winged wheel on a silver field; it symbolizes progress.

An eagle with its arms outstretched has a tape in its mouth with the Panamanian motto "Pro Mundi Beneficio" ("For the Benefit of the World"). Arcing over the eagle are nine gold stars that represent the nine provinces of Panama. On each side of the coat of arms are two gathered national flags.

National Flower: Holy Ghost Orchid

National Tree: Panama tree

National Animal: Harpy Eagle

Motto: "For the Benefit of the World"

Natural Environment

Panama is the southernmost Central American nation. It is on the Isthmus of Panama—a narrow strip of land with water on both sides that connects two larger bodies of land. The famous Panama Canal runs through the isthmus; this allows ships to pass from the Caribbean Sea on the north to the Pacific Ocean.

At its widest point, Panama is about 400 miles from west to east. At its narrowest point near the Panama Canal, it is only about 30 miles across. If you were to look at Panama from a satellite, you would see a landform that looks like an "S" lying on its side. There are many islands offshore.

Panama is in the tropics, and about one-third of it is covered with thick rainforest. There are low-lying areas along the coast. A spine of mountains and hills runs east and west almost the full length of the country. The peaks of the Panamanian chain were formed by volcanoes. There are extensive pastures and farmlands in the Azuero Peninsula in southern Panama.

There are about 500 rivers that cross Panama, but many cannot be navigated. However, the wide Río Chagres in central Panama is an important source of hydroelectric power.

Built across the center part of the Río Chagres is the Gatun Dam, which forms Gatun Lake. This artificial lake forms part of the Panama Canal and was once the world's largest man-made lake.

Plants and Animals

Panama means "place of abundant fish." Here you'll definitely find fish in the jungle pools, the offshore waters, and the freshwater lakes. But fish are just the tip of the iceberg!

Because of its hot and humid tropical environment, Panama is the most biodiverse country in Central America. More than 29 percent of the country is protected by an extensive national park and wildlife refuge system. What's unusual—and thrilling—is that you can go from a modern city to a primitive jungle in a fairly short trip!

The Darién Jungle (called the "darkest jungle") in the northern Darién province is the Western Hemisphere's largest tropical rainforest apart from the Amazon Basin. Most people travel through this thick jungle only by canoe. The indigenous communities that live there share it with lots of other living things. There are 2,000 species of tropical plants and a wide variety of animals like bushdogs, ocelots, armadillos, pumas, anteaters, monkeys, deer, *caimans* (an alligator cousin), the *capybara* (the largest rodent in the world), and many snakes. Panama also has several animal species found nowhere else, like the golden tree frog and the giant tree sloth.

Bush dog

The diverse bird population in the Darién includes the harpy eagle (Panama's national bird); colorful tropical birds like macaws, parrots, and toucans; and migrating birds that fly in from other areas. Imagine the symphony of bird sounds you would hear every day!

From the jungles in the northeast to the grasslands in the southwest, people grow corn, beans, and tuber crops like potatoes. Mangrove thickets grow in dense groves along the Caribbean and the Pacific coasts. (Mangroves are tropical evergreens that have long roots and stems.) There are banana plantations in the western deltas near Costa Rica.

Finally, Panama is paradise for tropical flower lovers! There are more than 1,000 species of orchids growing from the lowlands to the highlands. *Heliconias*, which resemble the brightly colored Bird of Paradise flowers, sprout in dense bunches along the streams and lakes. Artists the world over make their way to Panama each year to paint these botanical beauties.

Heliconias

Find the Secret Word

Below are six creatures you just read about that are found in the Darién Jungle. Write the name of each in the spaces at the right, and then write each boxed letter in the spaces at the bottom of the page. What's the secret word?

1.  ☐ _ _ _ _ _

2.  _ _ _ ☐ _ _ _ _ _

3.  _ _ _ _ _ ☐

4.  _ _ _ ☐ _ _ _ _

5.  _ _ _ ☐ _ _

6.  _ _ _ ☐

SECRET WORD: ____ ____ ____ ____ ____ ____

A History of Panama

Pre-Columbian Inhabitants

Panama has been inhabited for at least 10,000 years by dozens of indigenous groups prior to the arrival of the Spanish in the 16th century. The few architectural artifacts that have been found reveal that the early inhabitants were part of a trading zone that extended from Mexico to Peru. But people in Panama's indigenous communities today still tell tales of lost cities.

Spanish Settlers

Although Panama was discovered by Spanish explorer Rodrigo de Bastidas in 1501, his first mate, Vasco Núñez de Balboa, gets most of the credit. Balboa crossed the Isthmus of Panama and, in 1513, became the first European to reach the Pacific Ocean. Like so many other Spanish explorers, Balboa was in search of gold—something Panama definitely didn't have. He immediately claimed all of the land for the king of Spain.

Panama became a Spanish settlement—but not without its growing pains. In 1519, a cruel Spaniard, Pedro Arias de Ávila (called *Pedrarias*), founded the city of Panamá near modern-day Panama City. He had Balboa, who was his son-in-law, beheaded on a charge of treason. Pedrarias made Panamá a trade center and an important stop on a major trade route for Peruvian gold and silver, Oriental spices, and other treasures.

In 1572, Sir Francis Drake of England destroyed Nombre de Dios, a city on the Atlantic Panamanian coast that was another important stop along this route. He set sail for England with a ship loaded with Spanish gold. Drake essentially put Great Britain (and the world) on notice: the country of Panama was filled with riches!

More British explorers followed Drake and raided the entire country. British pirates burned the city of Panamá to the ground in 1671 and made off with its entire treasure. The Spaniards rebuilt the city a few years later just a few miles from the original site. You can still see the ruins of the old settlement within the city limits of present-day Panama City. In 1739, Admiral Edward Vernon destroyed the fortress at Portobelo on the Caribbean, which at the time was the greatest Spanish port in Central America.

The Break with Spain

Panama broke away from Spain in 1821. It joined a union of Colombia, Ecuador, Bolivia, Peru, and Venezuela, which was named the Republic of Gran Colombia. When the union dissolved in 1831, Panama remained a province of Colombia.

By this time, the world's super powers had discovered a large benefit in this small land. The Isthmus of Panama was the narrowest point between the Pacific and the Atlantic Oceans. The United States constructed a railway across the isthmus. During the California Gold Rush of 1849, thousands of people traveled from the east coast to the west coast of the United States via Panama so they could avoid the hostile Native Americans in the central part of the United States. The railroad made Colombia and Panama rich. It also sparked the first talk of a canal across Central America.

The Panama Canal

In 1878, the French got a contract from Colombia to build a canal. The French had recently and successfully constructed the Suez Canal in Egypt, which links the Mediterranean Sea and the Red Sea. However, they not only underestimated the effort in Panama, they also lost thousands of workers to yellow fever and malaria. By 1889, they had to give up on the project.

Panama seceded from Colombia in 1903. It then signed a treaty with the United States to construct the Panama Canal. It also gave the United States control over a strip of land on either side of the canal. (This is now called the Panama Canal Zone.) The U.S. Army Corps of Engineers built the Panama Canal between 1904 and 1914. The first ship sailed through it on August 15, 1914.

In the years that followed the completion of the canal, the U.S. military tried to get involved in Panama's political affairs. Many Panamanians rebelled against this as well as the U.S. occupation of the country. In 1964, an anti-United States protest left 27 Panamanians dead and some 500 injured. Today Panamanians commemorate this event as National Martyrs' Day (Día de los Mártires).

In 1977, an agreement was signed for the complete transfer of the canal from the United States to Panama by December 31, 1999. This included complete withdrawal of U.S. military forces from the country.

The Regime of Manuel Noriega

After the sudden death of Panamanian leader Omar Torrijos in 1981, Colonel Manuel Antonio Noriega quickly and brutally seized power. The military dictator was a former head of Panama's secret police and a former CIA agent. He created a Dignity Battalion in every town whose members arrested people who were not completely loyal to him. He was involved in drug trafficking with Colombian drug lords. He murdered his opponents and rigged elections. The Panamanians demanded his dismissal, protesting with strikes, demonstrations, and violence against the Panama Defense Forces.

Finally, with the help of the United States, Noriega was removed from office in 1989. By the end of that year, the entire Panama Canal, the area supporting it, and the U.S. military bases in Panama were transferred to Panama. Noriega surrendered to U.S. forces. In 1992 he was sentenced to 40 years in a Florida prison.

Expanding the Canal

Panama after Noriega is no longer a dictatorship. There have been three free, democratic, and peaceful elections. In 2009, Ricardo Martinelli, a wealthy businessman, was elected president for a five-year term.

In October 2006, Panamanians approved an ambitious plan to expand the Panama Canal by adding a third series of locks. Construction of the new locks, which began in 2007, will enable wider, longer vessels to go across the isthmus. This expansion will double the canal's capacity. The construction will be finished in 2014 for a cost of $5.3 billion.

Panama Today

Panama gets a great deal of its income from operating the Panama Canal, banking, insurance, flagship registry, and tourism. The Colón Free Trade Zone near the Canal's Atlantic entrance also generates a huge amount of money for the country. It offers services and facilities for importing, storing, assembling, repacking and re-exporting products from all over the world. It's also the second largest duty-free (no tax) tourist shopping area in the world, and draws visitors from all over the globe.

In 2006, Panama signed a free-trade agreement with the United States, which is helping to boost its economy. Nevertheless, about a third of the population still lives below the poverty level. President Martinelli pledged to encourage foreign investment in Panama and to help the poor.

In the meantime, Panama remains a fascinating land of contrast and variety. Where else could you explore the beach, the mountains, the rainforest, well-developed modern cities, and historic ruins—all in a few short days?

Daily Life

The Family Unit

The family unit is at the center of most Panamanians' lives. Family members support and help each other throughout their entire lives. This includes extended family, such as grandparents, aunts, uncles, and cousins. They all get together to celebrate special occasions like birthdays and holidays. Married children who live outside their childhood home still visit their parents frequently.

The family roles in Panama are still very traditional. The father is the authority figure. The mother has more of the responsibility for raising the kids. The boys in the family usually have more freedom than the girls. The girls are very closely supervised.

This culture highly values its children. A baby's baptism to welcome the child into the church and into the family is a major family event. Godparents (called *padrinos*) are carefully chosen since they are expected to help the child whenever needed throughout the child's entire life.

Urban Life

More than 70 percent of Panama's people now live in densely populated urban areas like Panama City. To accommodate the great number of people, the cities are packed with high-rise apartment buildings and condominiums. However, this is posing some problems. The population is increasing in many urban areas way beyond what was originally expected. The downtown streets are crowded with traffic, and sometimes there are power outages simply due to overload.

The Wealthy
A handful of Panamanians are extremely wealthy business owners. They usually live in single-family homes in exclusive neighborhoods. They have live-in servants, more than one car, and perhaps a second home elsewhere. Their kids usually go to private schools or study abroad. Exclusive real estate areas in Panama have also become popular places for international celebrities and movie stars to buy property.

The Middle Class
About one-fourth of the population has a middle-class income. This means they own an apartment or a home (probably in Panama City) with modern conveniences, and they probably have a car. Many middle-class citizens work for the government, the Panama Canal, or one of the foreign firms with an office in the country. Some people create goods for export.

The Lower Class
About one-third of Panamanians live well below the poverty line. They have little income and own no property. Many migrate to Panama City in search of employment. They end up working as day laborers or servants to the wealthy. The government has constructed thousands of small homes for these low-income people on the outskirts of the major cities. But their lives are very hard, and they have little hope of making more money in order to have a more prosperous life.

Rural Life

Five percent of the Panamanian population lives in the remotest parts of Panama, which includes the Darién Jungle. Most of these people are from one of Panama's seven indigenous tribes. Their way of life ranges from very primitive to somewhat westernized. Some speak in their native tongues and refuse to speak Spanish. Some live in regions that are so remote that there are no roads, and the children have no access to schools.

For many in the Darién Jungle, daily life means being connected to the often dangerous land. The heat and humidity are extreme. The common method of transportation is the canoe. Houses are likely to be open structures built on stilts with thatched roofs. Local residents hunt, fish, farm, gather firewood, and make medicines from local plants. They regularly deal with dangerous animals and poisonous snakes. Their music, dance, and traditions have been handed down through the generations. They are struggling to maintain their cherished way of life.

Are We There Yet?

In Panamanian cities, many people take buses called "red devils" *(diablo rojos)*. The bus owners paint them in bright colors, with pictures of their favorite celebrities or politicians. People also get around by taxi. But whether by bus or taxi, there are long delays during rush hour in getting from one point to another. So, everybody behind the wheel is on the lookout for a faster way to get someplace. This means a lot of people taking shortcuts—which makes driving hectic!

In the rural areas, people walk, use buses, or ride horses. In the remote jungle areas, it's common to travel by canoe.

Going to School

By law, Panamanian kids must go to school for nine years. The government provides free education, but the students pay for their supplies and school uniforms. Wealthier families usually send their kids to private schools in the cities. All kids go to school from March to December and have summer vacation in January and February.

The classes in Panama are not very interactive. This means that teachers give lectures, and the kids take notes. They have homework daily.

After school, Panamanian kids play sports, watch TV, surf the Internet if they have computers, do homework, or see friends. Panamanian kids in the rural areas will help out with chores like planting or harvesting.

After primary school, most kids go on to secondary school where they'll study at least ten subjects. Some secondary schools focus on academics to prepare students for university. Others focus on vocational training that teaches specific job skills. Many rural families simply cannot afford to send their kids to secondary schools, which are usually in the larger cities. They don't have the money for the transportation, the supplies, or the room and board it would take for the kids to live in town during the week.

Those who want to pursue higher education can go to one of the Panamanian universities or a private college or trade school.

Famous Panamanians

Rubén Blades (1948–) is Panama's most famous musician and one of the most famous people born in the country. Much loved throughout Latin America, he's best known for his work in Latin jazz. His song entitled "Patria" ("Fatherland") is considered the second Panamanian national anthem. He's also a lawyer, an actor, and a politician. In 1994, he ran for the presidency, and he was Panama's Minister of Tourism from 2004 to 2009.

Arizona Senator John McCain (1939–) was born in the Panama Canal Zone. This famous "zonian" was the Republican Party's nominee for U.S. President in 2008. He's had a long and successful career in politics and served honorably in the military. During the Vietnam War, he nearly lost his life and was a prisoner of war for several years.

Former Major League Baseball player Rod Carew (1945–) is also a zonian. He is Panama's most famous baseball player and one of the best players of all time. From 1967 to 1985, he played for the Minnesota Twins and the former California Angels (now the Los Angeles Angels of Anaheim). Throughout his impressive 18-year career, he was an All-Star 17 times and won seven batting titles. He has been a member of the Baseball Hall of Fame since 1991. In 2004, Panama City's National Stadium was renamed Rod Carew Stadium.

Retired boxer Roberto Durán (1951–) is one of the greatest boxers of all time. Born in Guarare, his nickname was "Hands of Stone."

Long-jumper Irving Saladino (1983–), called "Panama's Kangaroo," is a national hero. This incredible athlete from Colón is Panama's first Olympic gold medal winner (2008). When he arrived back in Panama after winning the gold at the Beijing Summer Olympic Games, the schools and offices in Panama were closed so everyone could welcome him home in Panama City.

Language & Expressions

Body Language and Etiquette in Panama
Here are some examples of body language and etiquette you'll find in Panama.

Drawing a circle in the air with an index finger means, "I'm coming right back!"

Wrinkling the nose means, "I don't understand!"

Getting someplace "on time" in Panama means getting there on "Panamanian Time." For example, bosses may allow their employees to get to work five to ten minutes late. There will probably be a 30 to 60 minute delay before a public event starts. People will probably arrive for a family event an hour after the stated start time.

The usual happy greeting in Panama City is "Buenas!" This means, "Good morning!"

It is common to ask for permission to take a commonly used object like a salt shaker—even if the person doing the asking already has the object in hand.

People do not take flowers (or anything else) as a gift for the host and hostess when invited to someone's home for a meal. Sometimes, however, they may ask in advance if they can bring anything.

It is customary to leave a little food on the plate when finished eating. This is called "the courtesy."

People often drop by each other's houses just to say hello—even at mealtimes.

People tend to dress formally for most occasions, despite the tropical climate.

Know Before You Go
Check out page 15 for some common phrases you will use in Panama. The spelling and pronunciation are also given.

FOODS

Panamanian cuisine is similar to that of other Latin American countries because it mixes influences from Africa, Spain, and its native people. However, the food is not very spicy. And much of it is cooked in oil.

Common seafood and meats include fish, lobster, *corvina* (a Pacific white fish), shrimp, chicken, and beef. Common fruits, vegetables, and grains include *plantains* (a starchy relative of the banana), corn, wheat, *yucca* (also called cassava, which has a starchy, edible tuberous root), beans, tomatoes, carrots, and cabbage. Rice is usually eaten twice a day.

Sweet cold fruit drinks *(chichas)* are served with lunch and dinner (and sometimes even with breakfast).

Daily Meals

Panamanians follow a typical meal schedule. They eat informally and at different times. Unlike families in other Central and Latin American countries, family members in Panama don't always gather together for dinner every evening. They reserve this for special occasions.

Breakfast is typically light and served between 6:00 and 8:00 AM. Since many businesses and schools start at 8:00, students and workers are likely to eat pretty early. Breakfast may include *hojaldras*—Panamanian doughnuts covered with sugar—cereal, fruit, or even a tortilla with eggs. On the weekends the family may have a brunch that lasts until noon.

Lunch is served between noon and 1:30 PM. This may be a hot meal with a meat dish, rice, plantains, or *empanadas* (see below). The evening meal is served between about 5:30 and 7:30 PM. This is usually the most substantial meal of the day. Like lunch, it will likely include rice, plantains, and a meat or seafood dish.

Favorite National Dishes

Panama is known for several national dishes that everyone eats regularly.

Ceviche
Ceviche is a raw seafood dish from Peru that other Latin American countries have adapted with their own finishing touches. The Panamanian version consists of white sea bass or other fish and octopus, shrimp, or squid. This is marinated in lemon or lime juice with chopped onions and celery, along with a fresh-tasting herb called *cilantro*. Panama's finishing touch is to serve it with little pastry shells *(canastitas)*. Ceviche is a common appetizer.

Fried Plantains
Fried plantains *(patacones de platano)* are another popular side dish. The plantain is a starchy relative of the banana that is not sweet or soft enough to be eaten raw. Unripe plantains are cut in half or cut into round "disks" and fried twice until they're a golden color. Then they're removed from the pan, pounded flat, and fried again! Plantains are a staple in Panama. They're usually eaten daily with steamed rice, meat, and beans.

Fried plantains

Empanadas
Empanadas are small, delicious turnovers stuffed with meat and cheese and fried or baked. In some Latin American countries, they're also filled with fruits or thick custards.

In Panama, empanadas are considered a snack, an appetizer, or a quick bite at lunch. They're usually filled with ground beef or shredded chicken and white or yellow cheese. In the port of Colón on the Caribbean, people fill empanadas with plantain puree, bake it, and call it a *plantain tart*.

Sancocho

Sancocho
Sancocho is a traditional Latin American chicken soup that is thick like stew. In Panama it's made with large pieces of chicken, yams and other vegetables, cilantro, oregano, onions, and garlic. Panamanians say that eating this flavorful soup on a hot day will cool you off.

Tamales
Tamales, seasoned filling boiled in banana or plantain leaves, are a worldwide favorite! This is particularly so in Panama, where you'll find them served at the holidays and for all other special occasions like weddings and birthday parties. Tamales in Panama are large and commonly filled with chicken, raisins, onion, tomato sauce, and sometimes sweet peas.

Tres Leches Cake
Tres leches cake (three-milk cake) is one of Latin America's most popular desserts, and it's certainly popular in Panama! This is a cake soaked in evaporated milk, cream, and sweetened condensed milk. It is extremely moist and delicious.

Holidays & Festivals

Martyrs' Day
January 9
This day of national mourning commemorates the January 9, 1964 Panamanian student riots. The riots began as a result of a clash between students and Canal Zone police officers over the right to fly the Panamanian flag next to the U.S. flag. Violence broke out when the Panamanian flag was accidentally torn during the conflict.

In the resulting three days of fighting, 21 Panamanians and four U.S. soldiers were killed. This tragic incident was a deciding factor in the United States' transfer of control of the Canal Zone to Panama. Two monuments in Panama City commemorate this event. Those who died are remembered and honored each year.

The Easter Season
Carnival (Five Days before Ash Wednesday)
Carnival in Panama is one of the biggest in all of Latin America. In addition to the costumes, masks, music, and dancing, Panama City actually closes down five days before Ash Wednesday. A young queen and her attendants, who have been chosen by charitable organizations, preside over the Carnival.

The other major Carnival celebration takes place in Las Tablas, the capital of the inland province of Los Santos. The city splits into "Calle Arriba" ("Street Above"—an area uptown) and "Calle Abajo" ("Street Below"—an area downtown). Each area attempts to outdo the other with its own queen, costumes, parades and floats, fireworks, music, decorations, and food.

No matter where they are during Carnival, Panamanians have a tradition called *mojaderas,* or getting drenched with water. Whether by fire hose, water balloon, or buckets of water, everyone gets wet!

Easter

Easter is the most important Christian holiday of the year. Panamanian Christians attend joyous church services followed by family get-togethers. Panamanians have their own Easter Bunny tradition. Kids are told that a painted rabbit called the *conejo* brings them eggs. Of course, they get chocolates and other goodies, too.

November Patriotic Holidays

Separation Day from Colombia in 1903 (The Official National Independence Day)	*November 3*
Flag Day	*November 4*
Independence Day, Colón City (Panama's Columbus Day)	*November 5*
First Call for Independence from Spain	*November 10*
Independence from Spain	*November 28*

The festivities for Independence Week tend to be pretty quiet. However, school kids have patriotic parades in most areas. Many businesses are closed on Flag Day. Students from grade school through university get a vacation the entire Independence Week!

The Christmas Season

The Christmas season in Panama is also the summer season. But the fun and excitement are certainly not dulled by the heat and sunshine! Christmas in Panama is filled with fun, food, presents, and lots of celebration.

Mother's Day and the Feast of the Immaculate Conception of the Virgin Mary (December 8)

Mother's Day kicks off the holiday season with a celebration of the birth of Mary, Mother of Christ. One feature of this special day is that little girls dress as angels or attach angel wings to their dresses.

In the weeks leading up to Christmas, a huge parade in Panama City features floats and local bands that get everyone into the holiday spirit. The floats are decorated in traditional Panamanian colors. People wear traditional dress. Everyone looks forward to hearing—and seeing—the drummers every year. They swing their drums around their necks a couple of times while marching, then pick up drumming where they left off. Thousands of kids from poorer areas will be guests of honor at the parade and receive gifts and candy.

On the coast of Panama City, a giant Christmas tree is lit. Everyone gathers around it to sing Christmas carols. This day ends with a Christmas boat parade followed by a fabulous fireworks display.

Christmas displays include setting up nativity scenes *(nacimientos)* around the community and in the home. Some nativities have been passed down through the generations. While some families have a Christmas tree, it's more traditional to display lights inside and outside the house.

Christmas Eve (December 24)

The actual Christmas holiday is celebrated on Christmas Eve. Everyone has lots of fun with family and friends before the Christmas feast begins at midnight. Traditional foods include chicken with rice, turkey and stuffing, and fruitcake. Of course, you can't forget the tamales bursting with chicken! Tamales are such a big part of Christmas tradition in Panama that families often have tamale-making parties at holiday time.

Just after midnight on Christmas Eve, when the feast begins, the spectacular fireworks display in Panama City begins, too. People then give each other their Christmas gifts.

New Year's Eve (December 31)

In many areas, kids burn *effigies* (little dolls) of Father Time at midnight. This burns away anything bad from the old year so the New Year can start fresh. Music, dancing, feasting, and fireworks round out this happy holiday!

Three Kings Day (January 6)

Three Kings Day, which is also called the Epiphany, honors the Three Wise Men who brought gifts to the baby Jesus. This is one of the biggest celebrations of the Christmas season when kids get gifts.

Creative Arts

Music, Dance, and Festivals

Panamanian music and dance blend Spanish, African, and Native American cultures. The result is a rich array of music and dance handed down through the generations. If you're looking for a cultural festival filled with music and dance, you'll find one in Panama! There are many during the year.

Típico: Panama's Folk Music

Popular Panamanian folk music is called *típico*. Although it's centuries old, people still love it. They go to festivals and clubs to hear the best groups, and they listen to it on the radio. Típico gets its distinctive sound from traditional instruments like the conga drum, the accordion, and the *güiro* (a hollow hand percussion instrument played by scraping it).

Guiro

El Tamborito: The National Dance

Tamborito means *little drum*. Originally a Spanish dance, *el tamborito* is the national dance of Panama. It combines dancing, singing, and drumming. Men and women in groups of six or more are led by a female singer who is accompanied by drummers and a chorus.

The native drums of Panama—the *caja*, the *puja*, and the *repicador*—are central to el tamborito. The drums are made of hollow tree trunks with tanned cowhide drum heads. Each drum is a different size and makes a different sound, from light and quick to low and booming. All three drums played together get the dancers—and everyone in the audience—moving!

Other Music and Dance Styles

In addition to el tamborito, there are many music and dance styles popular in Panama today. You will find most of these genres—like *salsa*, *reggae*, *calypso*, and *cumbia*—in other Latin American countries, too. Panamanians keep them alive at their regional yearly music festivals.

Festival de la Mejorana

The Festival de la Mejorana is one of the top cultural events in Panama. This annual five-day celebration takes place in the small town of Guarare, just outside of Las Tablas. The country's best folkloric groups show off their skills and help keep Panama's folklore alive. Named for the *mejorana,* a small guitar-like instrument, this festival is so traditional that only típico can be played during the five days. No other music is allowed anywhere in town.

In addition to music, there are processions, a parade that lasts for hours, cultural events, exhibits, singing, and dancing. The festival draws thousands from Panama and many other countries each year.

Folk Costumes

During Carnival and the many other folk festivals in Panama throughout the year, you'll always see people in traditional Panamanian dress.

La Pollera

La pollera is the women's traditional folk costume—a frilled and embroidered blouse and a long, full skirt. This costume evolved from the dresses of wealthy Spanish women in the 16th and 17th centuries who could not wear their heavy satins in the hot Panamanian climate. They wore typical servants' clothing, but dressed it up with lace, embroidery, and ribbons. Gradually, they added the hair ornaments and jewelry still worn today.

Several yards of fine white linen or cotton are used to make each costume. Designs like birds, flowers, fruit, or vines are embroidered onto the clothing. (The shoes will be the same color as the embroidery.) The cost of these beautiful works of textile art can be thousands of dollars.

El Montuno

El montuno is the man's traditional folk costume. This consists of a white shirt, usually black trousers, and a *sombrero pintado* (a traditional, brimmed Panama hat).

Traditional folk costumes

The Panama hat is legendary! Even though hats go in and out of fashion, the Panama hat has survived. They were originally made in Ecuador and shipped first through Panama before being exported to other parts of the world. Thus, the name "Panama hat" stuck. The hats are made of braided straw plant leaves. A well-made Panama hat is supposed to be able to hold water. One thing is certain—a well-made one can be expensive! You'll still see many men in the tropics sporting a Panama hat with traditional folk dress, with jeans, or even with a business suit.

Folk Art

Woodcarvings, ceremonial masks, baskets, and pottery are all key examples of Panamanian folk art. The Embera and Wounaan, who live in villages mostly in the Darién Province along the Pacific coast, are famous for their handicrafts, especially their baskets. These museum-quality beauties are some of the finest baskets in the world.

Wounaan basket

Perhaps the best-known Panamanian folk art is the *mola*. Molas are made by the Kuna women, many of whom live quiet lives on islands or in remote areas of Panama. *Mola* is the Kuna word for *blouse* or *shirt*. But the term now means the intricate embroidered panels on the front or back of a woman's blouse. This hand-made textile is created with a reverse appliqué technique. Several layers of different-colored cloth are sewn together. Then the design is created by cutting away parts of each layer. Finally, the edges of the layers are sewn down. Molas can take months to complete. The beautiful designs are inspired by Kuna legends and culture, as well as by modern illustrations.

Make a Simple Mola

Molas are some of the world's most beautiful folk art creations. Although the Kuna molas are made of fabric, you can get the same effect using construction paper. Follow the simple steps below.

Materials

- pencil
- several sheets of construction paper in different colors (8 ½" x 11" or 9" x 12" sheets)
- scissors
- glue

Directions

1. Decide what image you would like as the main figure on your mola. This could be an animal, a flower, a piece of fruit, or anything else you choose. It's best to keep the image simple.

2. Lightly draw this shape onto a piece of construction paper and cut it out.

3. Glue this shape onto a piece of construction paper that is a different color. Cut around your first shape, leaving a narrow border so the first image appears to be outlined by the new color.

4. Glue this entire image onto one large piece of construction paper.

5. Now draw shapes like stars, squares, or triangles on a piece of construction paper. Cut them out and paste them on a new sheet of construction paper, leaving a narrow border so each image appears to be outlined by a new color.

6. Paste these shapes onto your larger sheet around your main image.

7. You can fill in your background by cutting out thin lines and pasting them onto your paper.

Sports & Games

Sports

Many of the same sports that are popular in North America—especially football and baseball—are popular in Panama. Some Panamanian players have gone on to have successful careers in sports.

Baseball

Panamanians love baseball! The Panama national baseball team is currently ranked ninth in the world. During the season, Rod Carew Stadium in Panama City is packed with fans for the home games and for international baseball competitions. So many people attend baseball games that there are even plans to expand the current seating capacity in the stadium from 27,000 to 45,000.

Football

American football is starting to have a presence on the Panamanian sports scene. The U.S. forces in Panama played it in the Canal Zone, and many wealthier Panamanians over the years have sent their kids to American schools where they played American sports. Panama currently offers flag football and contact football leagues for kids who are ages eight and older. As a founding member of the Pan-American Federation of American Football, Panama has pledged to add many more youth and junior football programs in the coming years.

Football (soccer) is popular in Panama, too, as it is in every other Latin American country. Kids grow up playing soccer, and there are many school and club teams. Panamanians root for Panama's national football team, which has competed regularly in the FIFA (International Federation of Association Football) World Cup since the late 1970s.

Other Sports and Pastimes

Golf, tennis, and water sports like surfing, sailing, and fishing are all popular pastimes in Panama.

Panama Makes History at the Olympics

Irving Saladino gave Panama its first Olympic gold medal in 2008 at the Beijing Summer Olympic Games with his record-setting long jump. The "Panamanian Kangaroo" was the first athlete from Panama to win a gold medal. Prior to Saladino's win, Panama had not been able to bring home an Olympic medal since 1948!

Panama Fish Word Search

Panama means "place of abundant fish." Find them in this word search. The words can be listed across, down, or up.

AMBERJACK   MARLIN
BASS   ROOSTERFISH
BONITO   SAILFISH
DOLPHIN   SHARK
DORADO   SNAPPER
GROUPER   TUNA
JACK   WHALE
MACKEREL

G R O O S T E R F I S H

R D O R A D O Q R J S V

O S U G I A R H O A R S

U V B X L E R E K C A M

P K Q W F Z E I S K L A

E O F N I H P L O D T R

R B A S S W A Y N Y Y L

A O M B H E R G E E S I

T N R E P P A N S C E N

T I F R A A C W H A L E

U T S W N D S O A R R O

N O P I E B A L R T T Q

A M B E R J A C K V B W

Peru

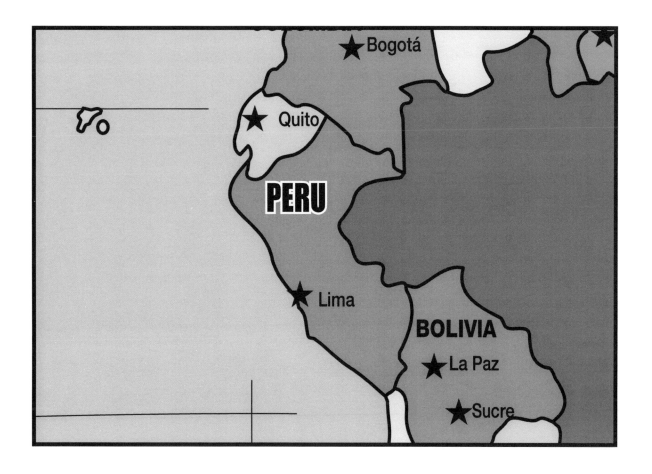

Welcome to Peru!

Peru was home to the legendary Incas, for whom it is probably best known. Although the country has had a lot of instability since it became independent in 1821, its rich cultural heritage survives *and* thrives! The Indians, Asians, Europeans, and Africans who live in Peru today honor each their own cultures. Yet, they have a strong national identity in one of the world's most beautiful and biodiverse lands.

After you have finished learning about Peru, be sure to check out page 148 for additional classroom activities.

FAST FACTS

Official Name:	Republic of Peru
Location:	Western South America. Peru is bordered on the north by Ecuador and Colombia, on the east by Brazil, on the southeast by Bolivia, on the south by Chile, and on the west by the Pacific Ocean.
Population:	29,546,963 (2010 estimate)
Capital City:	Lima
Area:	496,222 square miles. Peru is slightly smaller than the state of Alaska.
Major Language:	Spanish (official language) Quechua (official language) Aymara many minor Amazonian languages
Major Religion:	Christianity (predominantly Roman Catholic)
Currency:	The nuevo sol 1 nuevo sol = 100 céntimos
Climate:	Varies from tropical in the east to arid desert in the west and temperate to frigid in the Andes Mountains
The Land:	Western coastal plain, high and rugged Andes Mountains in the center, and the lowland jungle of the Amazon Basin in the east
Type of Government:	Constitutional Republic

Flag:

The flag has three equal vertical bands of color, beginning with red on the hoist side, white, and red. Depending on its use, it may have different emblems on it, such as the coat of arms.

Coat of Arms:		The coat of arms features a shield bearing a *vicuña* (the national animal) on a light blue background, the *cinchona tree* (the source of quinine, a drug that combats malaria) on a white background, and a yellow cornucopia spilling out gold coins on a red background. There are four variations of the Peruvian coat of arms, depending on its use, but all have these basic symbols on the same shield.

National Flower: Cantua buxifolia (called Cantuta—a flowering plant found in the forest along the eastern slope of the Andes Mountains)

National Tree: Cinchona

National Animals: Vicuña
Andean Cock-of-the-Rock

Natural Environment

The Coastal Plain
The west coast of Peru is a narrow, dry plain. There is rich farmland along the major valleys that are formed by the Andes Mountain rivers that drain to the west. The coastal waters are excellent fishing grounds.

About 40 percent of Peru's people live on the coastal plain. About 25 percent of the people in Peru live in the coastal capital of Lima.

Andes Mountains
The spectacular Andes Mountains run through Peru from north to south. They are composed of two large mountain ranges with snow-capped volcanoes and mountain valleys. They were home to the Incas, and they continue to be home to many of Peru's indigenous populations. The area is rich in minerals. About 50 percent of Peru's people live here.

In the central Western Andes is Nevado Huascarán, the highest point in Peru and in all the Earth's tropics. It is also the sixth-highest mountain in the Western Hemisphere.

In the southeastern Andes, on Peru's border with Bolivia, is Lake Titicaca, the world's highest navigable lake. The lake is the best-known geographical feature of the Altiplano Plateau, where the Andes are at their widest. Around Titicaca are the Uros, a group of 42 man-made islands of floating reeds. The islands were originally created to defend the country, and many of them still have watchtowers. Today, however, they're mainly a tourist attraction.

About 100 miles west of Lake Titicaca is Nevado Mismi. This isolated, high slope is the ultimate source of the mighty Amazon River.

Amazonian Rainforest
In the northeast is the tropical Amazonian rainforest that extends east and borders Columbia and Brazil. This flat jungle is the world's fourth-largest tropical forest. About 60 percent of the area of Peru is located here. It is also the source of three major tributaries of the Amazon River: the Ucayali, the Huallaga, and the Marañón Rivers. Only about ten percent of Peru's people live here.

Plants and Animals
Peru is one of the world's most biologically diverse countries. In all regions combined, Peru has more than 21,000 species of plants and animals. It has more than 1,800 species of birds alone—the second highest of any country on Earth. The Peruvian government has established more than 50 protected areas to preserve them. UNESCO (United Nations Educational, Scientific and Cultural Organization) has designated three national parks in Peru as World Heritage Sites.

On the dry west coastal plains are mainly desert shrubs, grasses, and tuberous plants that require little water for survival. The coastal waters and offshore islands are teeming with gulls, terns, albatross, and pelicans. The abundant sea life in the ocean includes sea bass, tuna, crab, lobster, and shrimp. Sharks and whales are also common in the South Pacific waters. Sea lions and penguins can be seen on the islands off the southern coast.

As you can imagine, the rugged and rocky Andes have relatively little plant life. The small amount of vegetation there survives on little water. This includes the mesquite tree, cacti, grasses, and eucalyptus plants. On the lower slopes of the Andes are steep forests in which mosses, orchids, and tropical bromeliads grow. The Highlands are famous for their alpacas and vicuñas. There are also deer, chinchillas, and *viscachas* (small rodents in the chinchilla family) in this region.

The Amazon Rainforest is thick with trees, plants, exotic tropical flowers, and vines. Here you will find mahogany, cedar, and rubber trees as well as the national tree, *cinchona*. Plants used for flavoring food, such as *sarsaparilla* (the flavoring used for root beer) and vanilla, are found here, too. Monkeys, jaguars, and pumas roam the rainforest. Macaws, parrots, and hundreds of other birds nest in the canopies of the trees. Giant anacondas, as well as many other snakes, lizards, and turtles are found here, too. Dolphins cruise the rivers, which are also home to piranha, alligators, turtles, and frogs.

A HISTORY OF PERU

Pre-Columbian Inhabitants

The legendary Incan Empire is the culture mostly closely associated with Peru. But the Incas are only a small part of Peru's history! Evidence shows there were people in Peru well before the Incas, around 9000 BCE. The Norte Chico civilization (the oldest known civilization in the Americas) lived along the Pacific Coast between 3000 and 1800 BCE. This was followed by other cultures, such as the Nazca and the Chimú. These cultures developed many art techniques such as kiln-fired ceramics and weaving.

The Incas

By about 1430, the Incas (the word means *kings*) were living around the southeastern city of Cusco, the Incan capital. Within 100 years, they had become the largest empire in pre-Columbian America. They conquered a vast territory from northwest Argentina to southern Colombia. Cusco became the richest city in the Americas, with temples actually covered in gold. The Incas also built many other mountaintop fortresses, including the famous (and still mysterious) "lost city" of Machu Picchu. This haunting site was only discovered in the 20th century. It is Peru's main tourist attraction today.

Machu Picchu

The Incas were an advanced culture that used farming techniques like terracing and irrigation. They had no money and no organized economy; instead, they exchanged goods and labor. In 1532, when the Incan Empire was at its most powerful, a war developed between Atahualpa, the Incan ruler, and his brother over who would lead the Empire. Atahualpa was the victor.

In that same year, Spanish conquistador Francisco Pizarro and his men arrived in the Incan Empire, looking for the gold and silver mines in the Andes. After holding Atahualpa captive for months, Pizarro assassinated him and kept the ransom he had been demanding in exchange for sparing the Incan leader's life. Despite the Incans' fierce fighting, Pizarro and his men seized Cusco, acquired a vast amount of gold and silver, and forced Spanish rule. The Incas continued to fight over the next several years, but the Spaniards prevailed.

Many of Peru's Native Americans today are descended from the Incas. Some still speak Quechua, the Incan language, or the related language of Aymara.

Colonial Peru and Spanish Rule

The Spanish founded the present-day capital of Lima on the Peruvian coast in 1535. Although indigenous Peruvian cultures tried to resist the Spaniards, they simply couldn't win against the Spaniards' guns, horses, and manpower. The Spanish Crown established the Viceroyalty of Peru, which included most of Spain's South American colonies.

The new rulers of Peru were born in Spain and appointed by the Spanish crown. Wealthy immigrants from Spain held the most important positions. They also got the land, including all of the land occupied by Peru's native people. Francisco de Toledo, the Spanish viceroy of Peru from 1569 to 1581, made silver mining the country's main industry. He forced the indigenous people to work the mines. The mines flourished until the 18th century when silver production dropped.

Stripped of their land *and* their rights, the indigenous people struck back. They were led in a full-out rebellion in 1780 by José Gabriel Condorcanqui, who fought under the name of his royal Incan ancestor, Túpac Amaru II. He had served the Spanish rulers while trying to improve the conditions of the enslaved native people, especially in the mines. But his rebellion was crushed. Amaru and the indigenous leaders were all cruelly executed in Cuzco. No one knows for sure whether any of the Incan royal line survived.

Independence

In the early 19th century, most of South America was fighting for its independence from Spain. General José de San Martín, one of the prime leaders responsible for South America's liberation from Spain, entered Lima in 1821 and declared it independent.

Simón Bolívar, another key figure in South America's fight for independence, had freed Venezuela, Colombia, and Ecuador. In 1822 San Martín and Bolívar met in Ecuador. No one knows just what they talked about, but Bolívar continued with the liberation of Peru. San Martín left Latin America for France. After numerous battles in the following years, Spain finally surrendered in 1826.

San Martín

Early Years of the Republic

Peru's early years as an independent nation were filled with power struggles among the leadership. There was a brief union with Bolivia that fell apart. From the 1840s to the 1860s, the country had gained economic stability by exporting *guano* (seabird droppings) and rubber. (Guano is used as an ingredient in fertilizer and gunpowder.) But by the 1870s, the resources had decreased, the country's economy was shaky, and the leaders were fighting among themselves.

Peru won a brief war with Spain in 1866 but was defeated by Chile in the War of the Pacific (1879–1883). As a result, Peru lost areas of the northern Atacama Desert that were rich with nitrate deposits, along with a large portion of its southern coast. Until well into the 20th century, Peru had border disputes with Ecuador that erupted in deadly fighting every few years. This was only resolved in 1942, and the Peru-Ecuador border has remained the same since then.

The Twentieth Century

Peru's history throughout much of the 20ᵗʰ century was shaped by military dictatorships and coups. One regime would begin some reforms, and the next regime would stop them. The country suffered much civil violence during the 1980s, in which about 70,000 people died in clashes between Peruvian armed forces and Communist party guerillas called the Shining Path. The goal of the Shining Path was to overthrow the democracy and institute a pure form of Communism.

The Shining Path brutally killed peasants, trade union organizers, elected officials, and average citizens. It is viewed worldwide as a terrorist organization. Since the capture and imprisonment of its leader by the Peruvian government, the group has been largely inactive.

Peru Today

Today Peru is experiencing more prosperity and peace than it has in decades. As of 2006, President Alan García (who was also president from 1985 to 1990) has been instituting reforms that are helping the economy grow. Peru now trades with the United States, China, Brazil, and Chile. Its main exports are copper, gold, petroleum, farm products, textiles, and fish meal. Foreign investors are beginning to discover this still somewhat mysterious land.

But Peru continues to struggle. In 2007, a massive coastal earthquake measuring 8.0 severely affected several cities, including Lima. (An 8.0-level earthquake causes extreme damage in areas several hundred miles across.) Many devastated areas have not yet been rebuilt. The cost of living has risen sharply, but salaries have not. The government is now allowing restaurants and land development near revered historic sites like Machu Picchu—a ruling that a lot of people oppose. Many in rural Peru are illiterate and have no access to healthcare or basic services like running water. The people of Peru have their work cut out for them. What the future holds for this beautiful land of contrasts remains to be seen.

Name _____   Date _____

The Intriguing Incas

The Incas are one of the world's most fascinating and most advanced civilizations. From about 1200 to the time they were conquered in 1533 by the Spanish, the Incas greatly expanded their territory and became the largest empire in pre-Columbian America.

Use Internet sites or other resources to read about this fascinating culture. Look up each of these subjects and write a couple of sentences telling what you find about each.

1. Who was the Sapa Inca? _____

    _____

2. How did the Incan government care for the common people? _____

    _____

3. Describe the Incan system of terraced farming. _____

    _____

4. Describe the Incan religion. _____

    _____

5. Tell about a few Incan inventions. _____

    _____

6. What did explorers find at the archaeological site of Machu Picchu? _____

    _____

7. What was an Incan roadrunner? _____

    _____

8. Tell a bit about the Incan road system and who was allowed to use it. _____

    _____

9. What two indigenous groups of people in Peru still strongly carry on the Incan cultural traditions, especially in the Andes?

    _____

10. Write or draw one other thing you found interesting about the Incas. _____

    _____

The Mysterious Nazca Lines of Peru

Read the passage below about the mysterious Nazca Lines. Then look at the images of the Nazca Lines at the bottom of this passage. What image do you see in each of these pictures? Write your answer under each picture.

Who doesn't love a good mystery? The Nazca Lines have provided plenty of that since their discovery in the early 20th century, when airlines spotted them as they flew across the Nazca Desert. Located in the desolate province of Nazca, one of the driest places on Earth, the Nazca Lines have inspired lots of good stories over the years.

Archaeologists have discovered Cahuachi, the city of line-builders, just south of the Nazca Lines. The city was built about 2,000 years ago, but the people left it 500 years after it was built. No one knows why. Researchers think the city was probably abandoned after natural disasters destroyed it. They also think that Cahuachi was a center for rituals and ceremonies.

There are hundreds of Nazca Lines in an area about 37 miles long and one mile wide. They range from simple lines scattered at random to complex figures—all of which took years to create. The lines were made by digging out furrows in the ground. The reddish pebbles of the desert soil contrast with the light-colored earth underneath. This contrast—light against dark—makes it easy to see the lines from the air. Since there is little climate change in this region, the Nazca Lines are virtually untouched by harsh weather and remain well preserved.

The Nazca Line designs include huge animals, plants, flowers, yarn, looms, and strange figures. Nobody really knows for sure what the lines were for. They could have been used in rituals to summon water. They could have been giant astronomical calendars. Some even think aliens created them and used them as runways for their spaceships! Whatever the real reason for their existence, the mystery of the Nazca Lines continues to fascinate us to this day.

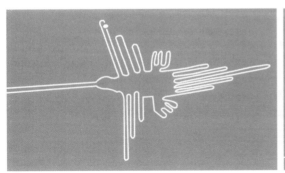  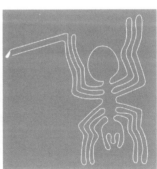

_____ _____ _____

Daily Life

The Family Unit

Peruvian society is very traditional when it comes to family and social roles. Men are expected to get married, have families, and provide for them—even though many women today work outside the home. Men generally have the most authority in the house, although women make decisions about the children and other family matters. Mothers and daughters do more of the childcare and household chores than fathers and sons. Kids are taught to respect and obey their elders.

The nuclear family unit is very important. Just which family members live in the same household is sometimes determined by income. A young married couple with little money, for example, may live in one parent's home until they can afford to move out on their own.

People in rural Peru maintain very strong ties to their large extended families throughout their entire lives—even if they move to the large cities.

Urban Life vs. Rural Life

Much of the way people live in Peru is determined by their social class and whether they live in the city or the country. The population of Peru's cities swelled during the last half of the 20th century when many people migrated from the mountains to find work in the cities. Many were poor and remained so, living in shantytowns on the outskirts of major cities like Lima. Migration has slowed since the 1990s, but there is still quite a different standard of living for those who have money and those who do not.

Urban Life
People of the upper-middle class lead very comfortable lives. Most middle-class Peruvians have live-in servants who are usually young women from the mountain areas. The servants will do the daily tasks of running the house, like cooking, cleaning, and gardening. The family may have several homes: one in the city, a second at the beach, and even a third in the Andes or in another country. Each home will be extremely well maintained. Socializing with friends and family is likely to include dining out in restaurants several times a week for a late evening supper. Get-togethers with friends and family for birthday parties, weddings, and baptisms are frequent.

Life is not so easy for the poorer urban residents who live on the outskirts of town. Their housing is often cobbled together with materials gathered from any source. They may not have indoor plumbing and may be forced to cook on kerosene stoves. These people lack the education to get employment that pays well. Thus, they often have to work two or three jobs just to make ends meet. They have little free time, although they will continue to socialize with extended family members.

Rural Life
Daily life in the rural areas depends on just what needs to be done. During planting and harvesting, people rise early, work long hours, and go to bed early. Much of the work will be done by the entire village working together. Mothers will even carry their babies in colorful *k'eperinas* (slings) on their backs while working in the fields.

In addition to farm work, women and girls will spin wool to be woven into clothing and blankets. Everyone will help repair tools, carry firewood, and haul water. Many rural families will not have modern conveniences like TVs, irons, or blenders.

Those who herd sheep, llamas, and alpacas also follow a distinct cycle each year. They certainly live a more isolated life than farmers do!

In either case, the entire village will share in every family's celebrations. Weddings, baptisms, festivals and religious holidays—all of them will be communal events with lots of food, dancing, and music.

Alpacas

Going to School

Education is free in Peru, and children from ages seven to 16 must attend grade school and high school. But many lower-class families keep their kids from attending public schools because they need the child at home to help with the work. Many upper-middle class families send their kids to private schools called *colegios* where the standards are very high and the work prepares them for university in other countries. The private Catholic schools throughout the country are especially highly regarded. However, the high cost of the private schools makes it impossible for many Peruvian kids to attend.

Teachers and educated people are highly respected in Peru. They are considered role models and are thought to be more cultured.

Levels of Education
There are three basic levels in the Peruvian educational system: nurseries and kindergartens (ages three to five), primary schools (ages six to 12), and secondary schools (ages 13 to 17). Many kids have to walk at least an hour each way to get to school. Some kids live so far away they may stay with a family in town and go home only on the weekends. Some are in such remote areas they may not make it to school at all unless there is a rural school nearby.

Peruvian students

Students who want to go on to higher education after high school first attend an *academia* to prepare. There is a national university in almost every major city in Peru. However, they can only accept a small portion of each year's applicants.

The School Year
Kids in Peru start in March and end in December. The seasons are reversed in the Southern Hemisphere, so summer vacation in Peru is January, February, and March.

In some areas where there is not enough classroom space for all students to attend at the same time, the kids to go school in morning, afternoon, and evening shifts that are four hours long.

Illiteracy in Peru
Many people in the very poor areas of Peru cannot read or write. They either do not have a school nearby, or they do not speak Spanish (the language in which classes are conducted). The government is working to raise the country's literacy rate overall, but students who speak a language other than Spanish still must become bilingual to attend school.

Famous Peruvians

The country's best-known literary figure is Mario Pedro Vargas Llosa (1936–). Primarily a novelist and essayist, Vargas Llosa is one of the world's leading authors. He has also been involved in politics all his life and ran for the Peruvian presidency in 1990.

César Abraham Vallejo Mendoza (1892–1938) only published three books of poetry during his lifetime, but he is considered one of the greatest poets of the 20th century. Some consider him second only to Pablo Neruda, Chile's famous Nobel Prize-winning poet.

Award-winning American actor Benjamin Bratt (1963–) was born in San Francisco, California. His mother is a Peruvian indigenous activist who was born in Peru and moved to the United States when she was 14. Bratt is most famous for his roles in the well-known TV show *Law and Order* and in many popular movies.

Language & Expressions

Here are some fun facts about verbal and nonverbal communication in Peru.

Famous Peruvian Proverbs

Here are five famous Peruvian proverbs. What do you think they mean?

Little by little, one walks far.
The continuous drip polishes the stone.
You won't catch trout without wetting your feet.
It is better to prevent than to cure.
Your heart is content when your stomach is full.

Body Language and Etiquette in Peru

Here are some examples of body language and etiquette you'll find in Peru.

Self-discipline is a core value of Peruvian culture. Controlling emotions is highly valued, especially among men.

People respect their elders and will frequently show this by doing things such as giving up a seat of a bus for an older person.

It is considered polite to address everyone you come in contact with, including shopkeepers and restaurant owners.

Natives of the Andes regions are often shy with strangers and make little eye contact.

Shaking hands is the most common form of meeting and greeting.

Foreigners might be addressed as gringo (for a man) and gringa (for a woman). This means foreigner and is not meant to be offensive.

If you want to photograph the locals, ask first! They will probably say yes, but they may also ask for a tip in return.

It's considered okay to show up half an hour to an hour after the stated start time of an event.

When invited to a person's home, people bring a small gift of flowers, sweets, chocolates, or cakes. But they don't bring anything too showy! Also, they don't give 13 of anything (like flowers). They don't give anything that is purple or black. (These colors symbolize religious ceremonies). They don't give knives or letter openers. (These symbolize cutting relationship ties.) They also don't give handkerchiefs. (These symbolize mourning.)

Know Before You Go

There are three key languages in Peru: Spanish, Quechua, and Aymara. There are also dozens of native Indian languages. If you visit Peru, however, Spanish will be the language of business. Check out page 15 for some common phrases you will use in Peru. The spelling and pronunciation are also given.

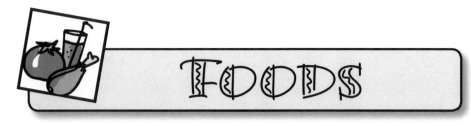

FOODS

Thanks to immigration from Spain, Africa, Japan, Italy, China, France, and Great Britain, Peru's cuisine is one of the world's most diverse, and, according to gourmets, it's one of the world's best! Lima alone is considered one of the fine-food capitals of South America, if not the world.

Peruvian cuisine is spicy. Chili peppers, along with a variety of herbs like mint, oregano, and cilantro, add heat, flavor, and color to many dishes. The biodiversity of Peru's plant life certainly extends to the crops grown in the country. There are about 650 native species of fruits; for example, 35 types of corn and 2,000 varieties of potatoes! Some of the foods like *quinoa* (a grain) are so rich in nutrients they're being used by NASA for astronaut food.

Daily Meals

Breakfast is the lightest meal of the day and often includes a quick cup of milk or tea and a piece of bread.

The key meal of the day is dinner, which is usually served around 1:00 PM. After dinner, people may take a short *siesta* (a nap) and then go back to work. Those who stay home may relax with personal activities or visit friends and relatives.

The late-night evening meal usually starts around 9:00 PM. Those in the upper-middle class might go to a restaurant for this evening meal several nights a week.

Common Foods

In every region of Peru, foods eaten on a daily basis will include spices, potatoes, rice, beans, fish, and grains like corn. But thanks to its very distinct landscape of coast, mountain highlands, and the tropics, various ethnic dishes that blend indigenous, Spanish, African, European, and Asian influences have developed in each area.

The Coast
Seafood abounds in the Pacific coastal waters. As a result, one of the country's favorite national dishes—*ceviche*—is extremely popular here. Ceviche is a delicious mixture of raw fish, shrimp, scallops, or squid marinated in a peppery lime mixture. This is typically served with sweet potatoes. Nearly every Peruvian restaurant in the larger cities will have its own special ceviche on the menu.

Ceviche

Street food vendors abound in the larger cities like Lima. It's easy to grab a quick snack of *anticuchos* (beef heart chunks marinated in spices and served on a stick) and *tamales* (corn mixed with meat and spices and wrapped in a banana leaf).

The Mountains
People of the mountain highlands eat the same types of foods their Incan ancestors did. This includes potatoes, rice, beef, chicken, pork (especially suckling pig), llama, and sheep. Corn is especially common. Dishes like corn on the cob with cheese are weekly treats. Soups are a highlander staple, particularly those with trout caught in Lake Titicaca.

One major component of the diet in this area is roasted *cuy* (guinea pig). Originally the indigenous people of the Andes used this in ceremonial meals only. Today it's a staple of the diet among people in the Andes highlands. Peruvians eat about 65 million guinea pigs a year. Families in both urban and rural environments raise them for extra income. It's common to see them sold at markets and fairs.

138

A special mountain feast that has existed since the time of the Incas is the *pachamanca*. Meats like pork, beef, sheep or guinea pig, along with vegetables, are cooked in a pit of heated stones. The stones and food are covered with grass and earth and allowed to cook for a couple of hours. The preparation and cooking time are long, but the result is delicious and feeds several people. Although pachamanca was once only a banquet dish of the Andes, now you can find it in some restaurants outside Lima.

The Tropics
The tropical Peruvian diet includes the many fresh fruits like kiwi fruit and pineapple, and vegetables available in the area like bananas and plantains (a starchy banana).

Rice is a common side dish and ingredient in many dishes. Lots of fish and wild game like boars, monkeys, pigs, and deer round out the menu.

Popular Beverages
Inca Kola is the country's most popular soft drink. It's yellow, sweet, fizzy, and is said to taste like bubble gum or a mixture of sugar and pineapple. It's so popular, in fact, that worldwide soft drink giant Coca-Cola® couldn't beat Inca Kola in popularity in Peru. So Coke bought a substantial share of the Inca Kola company in 1999.

A popular drink that some people compare to the fruit taste of Kool-Aid® is Chicha Morada. This is made from a base beverage of boiled purple corn with pineapple chunks, sugar, and ice added to it.

Lúcuma

The juice of the *lúcuma*, a subtropical fruit of the Andes that is also called *egg fruit*, is made into juice and shakes that Peruvians love. It is said to have a flavor like a mixture of maple and sweet potato. It's also made into the third most popular flavor of ice cream in Peru (after vanilla and chocolate).

Sweets and Snacks
There are more than 250 traditional desserts in Peru. Local plants and ingredients figure heavily into the recipes. Common sweet treats include ice cream flavored with prickly pear cactus and pumpkin fritters with molasses syrup. There are also many different types of puddings, baked goods with creamy fillings, fried dough with sweet syrups, thick cakes, and many others.

Popular snacks include peanuts, potato chips, raisins, pumpkin seeds, chocolates, and toffee. Snacks specific to Peru include large roasted giant corn kernels and fried plantain chips.

Holidays & Festivals

National holidays in Peru are so enjoyable for everyone that the celebrations often last several days. Everyone joins in with lots of food, get-togethers, observing customary rituals, wearing costumes, and playing sports like soccer and volleyball.

The Easter Season
Carnival (Weekend before Ash Wednesday)
Carnival in Peru, like Carnival throughout Latin America, is one big street party before the solemn season of Lent. Costumes and masks, music and dancing, face painting, floats, feasting, and even throwing water on each other are highlights of the celebration.

Easter Week
Some of Latin America's most impressive Easter celebrations happen in Peru, where many people take part in portraying the passion, death, and resurrection of Christ. The events of Easter week focus on fasting, prayer, and religious processions through the streets. Schools are closed this entire week so children can attend services with their parents.

One of the highlights of Easter week takes place in the central Andean city of Ayacucho, which is known for its large religious celebrations. On the evening of Good Friday, two days before Easter, a spectacular structure of 1,000 lit candles is carried through the streets. In Lima there is a big procession with statues of Christ and the Virgin Mary carried on platforms through the streets. People throw rose petals from their balconies onto the procession below as a special sign of respect.

Easter
On Easter, people traditionally celebrate with a huge feast called *doce platos* (12 dishes). Kids may get chocolate eggs and have egg-painting contests.

Battle of Arica (Flag Day)
June 7
June 7 was declared Flag Day by Peru's liberator, General Jose de San Martin. He created the design for the first flag of the Peruvian Republic. The Battle of Arica was fought on June 7, 1880, between Chile and Peru in the War of the Pacific. (Peru lost the battle as well as the war.) Peruvians proudly display the flag everywhere on this day.

Fiestas Patrias (Independence Day Celebrations)
July 28–29
This is one of Peru's most joyful and meaningful holidays. During the whole month of July, every home, school, and business flies the Peruvian flag. July 28 honors Peru's liberator, General José de San Martín. July 29 honors the Peruvian Armed Forces and the National Police. The whole country takes a break for the Independence Day celebrations since most schools and lots of businesses close for vacation during this time. Tourism increases with visitors from all over the world joining in the celebrations.

The big national party kicks off on the evening of July 27 with folk dancing, music, and feasting in city plazas and parks across Peru (especially in Lima). Country fairs with horse shows and fireworks are also a big part of the celebration.

The morning of July 28 begins with a 21-cannon salute and flag-raising all over the country. The Peruvian president gives a state of the country address. If a new president has been elected, he or she will assume the duties of office on this day and give an inauguration speech.

On July 29, representatives of the Peruvian Armed Forces and the National Police parade throughout the main streets of Lima, which are decorated in Peru's national colors. Major military weaponry is displayed.

All Saints' Day and Day of the Dead
November 1–2
This two-day holiday celebrates love for the living and love for those who have passed away. It also incorporates elements of the Incan tradition in which mummies of the dead were present at important Incan rituals and ceremonies.

November 1, Day of the Living, is a time for friends and relatives to get together and enjoy a traditional meal of roasted pork and tamales.

November 2, Day of the Dead, is a time to honor friends and relatives who have died. The day starts with a special religious service. Then everyone heads to the cemetery with flowers and food to symbolically share with the deceased at the grave. People celebrate loss, but they celebrate life, too! The atmosphere can be joyful, with kids cleaning off gravestones and replacing old flowers with new. Relatives will stay at the cemetery, holding a candlelight vigil.

The Christmas Season
The Christmas season in Peru is also the summer season, so the excitement of shopping in outdoor markets in the warm sunshine adds to the holiday fun. Homes, businesses, churches, and schools all decorate with Christmas colors.

Large and small manger scenes are very much a part of everyone's holiday displays. The Quechua Indians are known for carving nativity scenes from wood or soapstone. However, the figures are shown in the clothing styles from the time of the 16th century conquistadores. The Three Wise Men may be accompanied not with camels, but with Peru's native llamas. Other figures in the scene might be a flower seller or a tamale vender—much as you would see in any Peruvian city.

Christmas Eve (December 24)
Christmas Eve is called *Noche Buena* (Good Night). In Lima and other large coastal cities, kids get a children's party on Christmas Eve. They place their stockings near the manger scene in their home, and Santa fills them while the family is at church. When the family returns from church, they place the figure of the baby Jesus in the manger, and the kids open their gifts. Fireworks traditionally end the Christmas Eve celebration.

Peruvian nativity

Christmas Day (December 25)
Christmas dinner traditionally includes turkey, baked potatoes, salads, tamales, hot chocolate, and fruitcake. In Lima, where the Spanish first celebrated Christmas in Peru in 1535, the celebrations include a bullfight and a procession with the statue of the Virgin Mary.

New Year's (December 31–January 1)
Many families celebrate the New Year by eating lunch or dinner together. There are no specific foods associated with this holiday. But Peruvians have some wonderful traditions and rituals designed to put the old year behind them and bring good luck and prosperity in the New Year.

Dressing up a doll with one's old clothes and then burning it symbolizes getting rid of the old and making way for the new. Eating 12 grapes at midnight on New Year's Eve—one grape for each month of the year—is said to bring good luck in the next 12 months. People put beans in their pockets at midnight or throw rice around the house to bring money and luck. Lighting colored candles in the house (yellow for luck, red for love, and green for money) is popular. In one annual ritual called *baño de flores* (bath of flowers), people fill a basin with water and flowers of a certain color (like red roses for love). They will then wash with the water, hoping to get what they wished for.

Three Kings Day (January 6)

Three Kings Day, also called the Epiphany, is the last day for the parties, dances, and processions of the Christmas season. This day honors the Three Wise Men who brought gifts to the baby Jesus. Traditionally, people dressed as the Three Wise Men bring gifts to children. Everyone eats *rosca de reyes* (kings' ring)—a sweet, round bread decorated with candied fruit that looks like a king's crown.

Festivals

Peruvians pack their year with nonreligious and religious festivals. Just about any time is a good time for celebration with music, dance, feasting, and fun. Sometimes the festivals, like Carnival at Lent, go on for days. Depending on the area of the country where the festival takes place, the costumes will depict indigenous cultures like the Incas, or they may poke fun at the Spanish conquerors.

Other than Carnival, the most famous festival in Peru is *Inti-Raymi*, or Festival of the Sun. This festival takes place in the former Incan capital of Cusco all during the month of June. The Incan culture based its religion on the worship of the sun, which they called *Inti*. This festival continues the Incans' honor of the bond between the sun and the earth. The high point of the festivities takes place on June 24. The ceremony starts early in the day at Koricancha Square in front of the Santo Domingo Church, which was built over the ancient Incan Temple of the Sun. The *Sapa Inca* (the Incan Emperor) calls on blessings from the sun. Then all participants, who are elaborately dressed as Incan priests, court officials, and nobles, move in a procession to the ancient fortress of Sacsayhuamán in the hills above Cuzco. Thousands of people from all over the world came to Peru each year to see this beautiful ceremony.

Temple of the Sun

Creative Arts

Music

Folk music predominates in Peru—particularly in the Andes where the Quechuas and Aymaras live in areas that were once part of the Incan Empire. Peruvian folk music has its roots in the music of the Andes and the music of Spain. Whether the music is soft and slow or lively and danceable, you can almost feel the high mountains and open spaces in the music. Three instruments give Peruvian folk music its distinctive and easily recognizable sound: the *siku*, the *charango*, and the *chajchas*.

The *siku* is the Andean panpipe. The reedy sound on this ancient musical instrument comes from the hollow bamboo from which it is made. Each region in the Andes has developed its own style of playing, with its own special shape, size, and method of tuning the instrument. Some Andean pan pipes are up to four feet long.

The *charango* is a small South American stringed lute traditionally made with the dried shell of the back of an armadillo. (Today they're made of wood.) This instrument is a direct descendant of one of the guitar-like instruments brought over by the Spanish in the 16th century. It looks like a ukulele. Several popular music groups, like the Gipsy Kings from France, feature the charango.

A traditional percussion instrument is the *chajchas*—a cluster of dried goat hooves sewn into a length of fabric. They are held in the hand like a shaker, or worn as a bracelet or anklet. The goat toes make a soft rattling sound.

Pan pipes

Dance

Marinera is the national dance of Peru and the most popular traditional dance. In this graceful reenactment of a courtship, the dancers use handkerchiefs as props. In the city of Trujillo, a national marinera contest is held each January. Although Peru, Africa, and Spain each claim to have developed the marinera, the dance blends influences from all three. There are marinera dance schools all over Peru. Different styles of the dance exist. One of the most interesting styles contains a part in which a horse rider on a Peruvian paso directs the *horse* to do the dance!

Other Peruvian dances developed over the centuries represent historical events, religious beliefs, farming work, or hunting. Usually the dancers wear costumes and masks. In one Andean dance called the *chukchu*, for example, the dancers represent laborers in the Colonial era that worked on the sugar plantations in the jungle but came back to the mountains with malaria and yellow fever. The "sick" dancers fall to the ground in pain and are treated by dancers dressed as doctors and nurses bearing medical instruments like giant syringes.

Folk Costumes

In the larger cities like Lima, people dress in the same way as people in any westernized country. However, especially in the rural mountain areas, people wear traditional clothing that is brightly colored and distinctive. Each region has its own hats, ponchos, skirts, belts, and blouses. It's often easy to tell which village a woman comes from just by the hat she wears. Often the women will wear three or four (or as many as 15) colorful skirts tied around her waist. Usually the clothing is made in the area.

Folk costumes

Peruvians created one of the most famous articles of clothing ever invented: the *poncho*. Worn throughout the world, the poncho is one sheet of fabric with an opening for the head. Particularly in the Andes, people still wear ponchos that are handmade from alpaca fiber just as they were hundreds of years ago.

Folk Art

In all of Latin America, Peru is perhaps the country best known for folk art. Its folk art not only keeps a cultural tradition alive, but it also provides whole communities with much of their annual income. Three of the most famous types of Peruvian folk art are *textiles*, *retablos*, and *gourd art*.

Textiles

Textiles have always played an important part in the life of Peru. In the ancient societies, particularly in the Incan Empire, clothing indicated social status. Special fabrics were used for sacred ceremonies. The fabrics were made with great skill, incorporating sophisticated designs.

Peruvian textiles today are still made with great skill and care. People all over the world eagerly buy the blankets, quilts, belts, ponchos, hats, scarves, finger puppets, and other items that are knitted, woven, or sewn with handspun fibers.

Retablos

A *retablo* is a wooden box that contains small wooden figures. Retablos were first brought to Peru by the Spanish explorers who created these tiny religious altars to take with them on their world travels. The people of the Andes adapted this art form, creating retablos that contain figures from their every life, traditions, and holidays. Master crafters in Peru use the same simple wood tools and modeling plaster as their ancestors did to create the colorful figures in boxed scenes.

Peruvian textiles

Gourd Art

For several thousand years, Peruvian folk artists have been producing some of the world's most intricate *gourd art*. Gourds are related to the pumpkin. They grow in a variety of shapes and sizes that lend themselves to be used as bird houses, bowls, toys, baskets, and many other useful items.

Each gourd is hand-selected, and the outer green skin is scraped off to reveal the lighter color underneath. After the gourd has dried in the sun, the artist sketches a pattern on it and then carves the pattern into the gourd with simple tools. Then the artist uses a technique called *pyrography*, which is essentially burning the wood to create shades of brown and black on the gourd. Some gourds are painted as well. Then, depending on how the gourd will be used, it is cut open, cleaned of its inner seeds and fibers, and coated.

Making Finger Puppets

One of Peru's most famous and fun folk arts is the finger puppet. Follow the directions below to make your own finger puppets. Consider making a group of puppets with a common theme, like family members, favorite animals or pets, favorite characters from a movie, or your favorite actors or singers.

Materials

- pictures for reference (people or animals)
- an old glove (knitted or fabric) or an inexpensive white craft glove available from your local art store
- scissors
- glue and narrow strips of ribbon for finishing the edge
- yarn (for hair)
- small buttons or sequins for the eyes and noses
- felt for the mouth
- optional: glitter, wood, seed, or plastic beads

Directions

1. If you're using pictures for reference, choose a few that will easily show the facial features of each person or animal.

2. Cut the fingers off of one glove. This can be an old glove you no longer use, or an inexpensive white craft glove available from your local art store.

3. Glue a thin strip of ribbon around the base of each puppet to prevent the fabric from unraveling.

4. Using your pictures for reference, decorate your finger puppets, or simply use your imagination!

5. Optional:
   - Write a story about two or more of your puppets.
   - Write a dialogue between two of your puppets.
   - Write a poem about one of your puppets.

Sports & Games

Sports

Peruvians love sports and they often paint their faces red and white to show support for their country. Football (soccer) is the major sport, and Peru has shown its true colors to the world. Peru has competed in four FIFA (International Federation of Association) football cups. Although it hasn't been able to qualify against football giants Brazil and Argentina since 1982, that doesn't stop everyone in the country from cheering on their favorite teams.

Of the four medals Peru has won at the Summer Olympic Games, three have been in shooting (1948, 1984, and 1992) and one was in women's volleyball (1988). Surfing, sailing, and tennis are all popular sports as well.

Bullfighting

Bullfighting is second only to football in its popularity. Bullfighting draws enormous crowds in Peru. The object of a bullfight is for the matador to subdue and kill one or more bulls by performing maneuvers at close range. It is a highly-dangerous sport and a highly-controversial one. Animal rights groups argue against it because the animals suffer. Others argue that is an important cultural tradition that should be continued.

Bullfight

In Peru, bullfights are held on Sundays and holidays. The oldest bullring in the Americas is the world-famous Plaza de Acho in Lima that can hold up to 13,000 people at one time. There are 55 other bullrings in Peru.

Games

Chess is the most popular indoor game in Peru. Children learn how to play this game at an early age. The legendary Julio Granda is a Peruvian national hero who has been playing chess since age five and has been a Chess Grandmaster since age 19. He is a five-time chess champion in Peru (most recently in 2002). He has also played in the biennial international Chess Olympiad nine times since the mid-1980s.

"Tiles" (Peruvian Hopscotch)

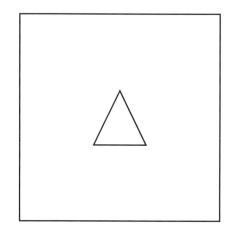

Number of Players Needed

5 to 10 or more

Materials

- chalk
- a small stone

Directions

1. Draw a large square in an open area, like a playground.

2. Draw a triangle in the middle of the square. The smaller the triangle, the harder the game.

3. Each player stands at least five feet from the square and takes a turn at throwing the stone.

   o   If the stone falls inside the triangle, the player gets a point and gets to toss the stone again.

   o   If the stone falls outside the triangle, the player loses his or her turn and the next player steps up to toss.

4. You can go as many rounds as you choose. Whoever gets the most points is the winner.

In Your Classroom

These additional classroom activities provide a hands-on way for your students to learn more about Latin America. These cross-curricular activities can be applied to any of the countries discussed in the book.

- To learn more about maps and globes and what they can tell us, have the students look at a wall map of the world or a globe and locate Latin American countries, including Argentina, Brazil, Chile, Cuba, Nicaragua, Panama, and Peru. Use a globe that shows country areas in terms of their true proportional sizes. Introduce students to the idea that seasons in the Southern Hemisphere are the reverse of our own—when it is winter in North America, it is summer in South America. Use a unit of measure, like a length of string, a ruler, or a hand width, to get an idea of each country's size, north to south and east to west, relative to other countries of the world. Compare the distance of various countries of the world to Cuba. Measure the distance from São Paulo and Rio de Janeiro to your city, and find other cities of different countries in the world that are an equal distance from your city. Encourage older students to use an atlas to locate other Latin American countries and find out more about their natural features.

- Invite your students to create a travel brochure for a tourist destination in one of the countries.

- Write on chart paper all the words the students can tell you about the rainforest. Take about five minutes to brainstorm the words. As a group, classify the students' rainforest words into "plant," "animal," "ecosystem," and so on. Use this list to structure your lessons. At the end of the rainforest unit, try this brainstorming and classifying exercise again. You'll be amazed by the growth of knowledge and understanding of both you and your students!

- You can show the power and fragility of the jungle ecosystem by making soda bottle terrariums. To make a terrarium: Rinse one liter plastic soda bottles and tops. Using a funnel, pour potting soil up to the top of the colored plastic bottom of the bottle. Drop in carrot seeds (for the fluffy fern-like plants of the rainforest) and bean seeds (to simulate the strangler vine and the tall growth trees). If you have some flower seeds, try them too. The Amazon Rainforest has more varied plant life per acre than any other place on earth. Your classroom bottles can approximate the richness of the rainforest. Add about one-eighth of a cup of water. Screw the top on tightly and LEAVE IT. Within an hour, the water cycle will be working, and your ecosystem will be going.

  The students can note plant growth by taking daily measurements on the outside of the clear bottle. They can check on the water cycle by moving their terrariums into the sun and then into the shade. They will see the condensation form inside the bottle, and then watch as the water drops fall back down into the miniature rainforest. Ask what would happen if the top is unscrewed, if you added a lizard, or if you put the bottle into constant light or constant darkness. Practice prediction and observation skills as the soda bottle jungles begin to thrive. Displaying the bottles on the window ledge provides a regular example of how all the parts of an ecosystem are connected. Talk about how the rainforest helps the whole earth's ecosystem as it continues to function as a closed environment. Talk about each bottle as the earth's atmosphere. The plants change carbon dioxide into oxygen, and the Amazon rainforest sends fresh air out to the whole world. Ponder what will happen if the rainforest is completely gone—not just the animals, bugs, and flowers, but the oxygen makers, too. When you are finished learning about the rainforest, plant the seedlings in a larger, less confining space. Note the difference between the warm, sheltered, soon-over-crowded "jungle" and the more open "garden."

- Have each student keep an Explorer's Journal. Make the cover as a tissue paper collage to emphasize the textures and colors of the rainforest. Add pages for terrarium measurement notes, drawings of the rainforest layers, personal feelings about the ecosystem, the creatures of the rainforest, and research notes. Each student can organize his or her learning by recreating it within the journal. This is an appropriate project for all ages and makes a great memento of a rainforest unit.

- Make a walk-through mural to create the sights and atmosphere of a real rainforest; include the grandeur of its high trees and the intricacy of its food webs. Let the students explore books you have brought in or that they have found in the library. Decide what part of the room should be the rainforest, and where the layers will be. The students will want to draw or make what they've been studying. You can cover the walls with paper and staple or tape on their pictures. Hang the creatures on strings to enhance the ecosystem effect. You can have a colorful and realistic rainforest—minus the bugs and mud!

- Have the students research, either individually or in pairs, a creature of the rainforest, thus becoming the "experts" for the class. Each report should include which layer the creature belongs to, what its part is in the food chain, and how it fits into the ecosystem. Have the students include the creature's vital statistics of size, color, and unique characteristics. After research is complete, each student can make his or her chosen creature. Take large butcher block paper, measure it to scale, and fold it over so that each student has a double sheet. The student can then draw the shape of the animal, bird, insect, or whatever creature he or she has chosen. Then the student can paint or color it, cut it out, and stuff it. Staple the open sides together. These creatures are now three-dimensional!

- Have your students create a timeline featuring the main events in the history of each country studied. Students can work together to create one large timeline, or in small groups to create timelines for each individual country.

- Discuss with your students the groups of people who are a part of their class, community, and nation. Investigate the origins of these groups. Did their ancestors come from other countries? Identify these countries.

- Ask the students to bring pictures of their family members to class. Discuss the role of grandparents in our families, and how this might differ from the role of grandparents in Latin America.

- Ask students to observe their community and report back to the class on the ways in which we decorate our communities and homes. Cut out squares of brightly colored paper or cardboard, and have the students design individual mosaics or a mural designed by the whole group. Discuss the idea of poverty with the students. In what ways are poor people the same as wealthier people; in what ways do they differ?

- Do simple math and counting games in Spanish. Play bingo using the Spanish numbers. Then try the activity using Portuguese numbers.

- Many Latin American cultures have their own proverbs. With your students, make list of familiar proverbs. What do these proverbs mean? Are they similar to any of the Latin American proverbs?

- Latin Americans use a rich body language along with their words. For example, "thumbs up" is used as a greeting and also means 'O.K.' and 'thanks'. Explore with your students the body language and sign language they use with their words. List on the board the languages the students have heard before and the languages spoken in their homes, among family members. Invite a Spanish speaker to come to class. Tape the interaction with the class so that the students can listen again. Keep an English-Spanish dictionary in the classroom and have the students label items in the room with their Spanish names.

- Many Latin American countries share similar cuisines. Divide the class into small groups, and have each group create Venn diagram comparing the foods of two Latin American countries. A Venn diagram comparing North American and Latin American cuisine can also be created.

- Visit an open market or farmers' market in your area. Talk about the items for sale and where they come from. Do any items come from Latin America, such as bananas or Brazil nuts? From other parts of the world?

- Set up a fruit juice bar in the classroom. Bring in a variety of fresh fruits and let the students experiment with different combinations and experience new taste sensations. To start with, put a small amount of water or milk in the blender, and then have fun trying different combinations of fruits. Chart the types of fruit juices your students create; make a graph to show which ones the class likes the best. Coconut and coconut milk are used in many Brazilian drinks and recipes. You can make fresh, grated coconut with your class to try on its own and to include in your different juices.

- Study the foods found in the Amazon rainforest. Bring in samples of coffee beans, chocolate (milk, semi-sweet, unsweetened, cocoa), and sugar (raw, brown, and white). Let the students explore the differences between the weak pecan shell of the temperate forest and the tough Brazil nut shell. Don't use paper plates and save another tree. Try cracking open the Brazil nuts, a great exercise in fine motor muscles. Using dark, light, and raw sugars, give the class an idea of the varieties of sugar.

- Choose one of the many Latin American holidays and celebrate it in your classroom! Have students create decorations and hang them around the room. Invite families to provide a snack or beverage for the occasion. Encourage students to dress for the festivities.

- Hold a class Carnival. Divide the class into samba groups. Each group can choose its own colors and theme. Students can plan their costumes, masks, and themes, work up their own dance routines based on their selected theme, and make up a song to accompany their performance. On the day of the class Carnival, students can dress in clothing that includes the group colors, and each group can take turns performing for the others. Percussion instruments will add to the gaiety.

- Have the students create their own class rap or a rainforest rap. As they create their rainforest rap, they may want to emphasize the animals, the layers, the colors, the smells, or the endangerment of the rainforest. String all their lines together with a beat, and rap it out. This can also be done with any of the specific countries studied.

- Put on a show of samba dancing with the accompaniment of your own homemade instruments. Record the show, and present it to parents and other students during Open House.

- During outside activities, have your students learn a few soccer fundamentals. Soccer is good for body movement and coordination. Everyone can join in and enjoy a game. Conduct a few simple drills that can be made into games. From a starting line, have students run and kick (dribble) the ball around a cone or other object about 50 feet away and dribble back to the starting line. Use one cone for each contestant. The first to return wins. A team of several students can each perform the same drill as a relay—each student dribbles the ball around the cone, returns to the starting line, and passes the ball to the next student on the team who then dribbles around the cone, and so forth. A non-competitive, cooperative form of the game will have the whole group working to reduce the time necessary for them to complete the relay. Hold a "World Cup" soccer match, and invite other classes to join.

- Make kites and decorate them with images of Central and South America. Display them in the classroom.

Answer Key

Argentina

Estancia Math (page 13)
1. 18 hands (72 ÷ 4 = 18)
2. 12 hands (48 ÷ 4 = 12)
3. 13 hands (52 ÷ 4 = 13)
4. 17 hands (68 ÷ 4 = 17)
5. 16 hands (64 ÷ 4 = 16)

Brazil

Creatures of the Amazon (page 30)
1. manatee
2. jaguar
3. iguana
4. capybara
5. spider monkey
6. poison arrow frog
7. sloth
8. macaw
9. alligator
10. mosquito
11. armadillo
12. piranha
13. rhinoceros beetle
14. toucan
15. anaconda

Take a Trip to Iguaçu Falls (page 34)
(There are 15 errors in this passage.)

Iguaçu Falls, which lies on the Brazil/Argentine border, is one of the world's most spectacular sites. Iguaçu means *big water* in the Tupi Indian language. And big it is! The 296 cascades in the shape of a horseshoe that make up the Falls span more than two miles across. Once you've seen the Falls, you will never forget the tons of water rushing off the cliffs and the mists rising from the jungle below.

One of the best ways to experience the Falls from the Brazilian side is to take a boat trip to get next to and sometimes under the falling water. You first board a truck that takes you through the jungle to the dock where you then board a boat. You put on your raincoat and life preserver and tuck your valuables into a plastic bag. Imaging your excitement as you navigate through the rapids, listening to the crashing water mixed with the roaring of the boat motors. The sound is so loud, you can't hear yourself talk!

The captain knows the rapids well. He or she dips the boat into the water a few times just to soak the passengers! The river is rocky, so you won't cruise too close to the big falls. But you'll be able to cruise under some of the smaller ones. And you won't even notice that you're thoroughly soaked—despite your raincoat. But who cares about getting wet when you're experiencing one of the most breathtaking places on the planet?

Cuba

The Case of Elián Gonzáles (page 76)
1. He left in a small boat.
2. His mother and 12 others.
3. His mother and ten others died due to the bad weather and the failure of the boat's motor. Elián and the other two survivors floated on an inner tube until they were rescued and turned over to the U.S. Coast Guard.
4. To his paternal great-uncle, Lázaro González.
5. Answers will vary.
6. They defied the order.
7. The INS (Immigration and Naturalization Service) raided the home and took the boy in the early morning hours.
8. Andrews Air Force Base in Washington, DC.
9. It ruled that Elián was too young to file for political asylum. His relatives had no legal standing. Only his father could speak for him. (His father wanted him back in Cuba.)
10. Answers will vary.

Nicaragua

Find the Secret Bird (page 93)
1. MUSCOVY DUCK
2. SPECTACLED OWL
3. KISKADEE
4. TROPICAL KINGBIRD
5. GREY GULL
6. ROYAL TERM
7. SNOWY EGRET
8. LIMPKIN
9. ALTAMIRA ORIOLE
10. BLACK HAWK EAGLE
11. SNAIL KITE
12. WHITE SINGED DOVE
The secret bird is: SCARLET MACAW

Panama

Find the Secret Word (page 113)
1. parrot
2. armadillo
3. toucan
4. anteater
5. caiman
6. puma
SECRET WORD: Panama

G	R	O	O	S	T	E	R	F	I	S	H
R	D	O	R	A	D	O	Q	R	J	S	V
O	S	U	G	I	A	R	H	O	A	R	S
U	V	B	X	L	E	R	E	K	C	A	M
P	K	Q	W	F	Z	E	I	S	K	L	A
E	O	F	N	I	H	P	L	O	D	T	R
R	B	A	S	S	W	A	Y	N	Y	Y	L
A	O	M	B	H	E	R	G	E	E	S	I
T	N	R	E	P	P	A	N	S	C	E	N
T	I	F	R	A	A	C	W	H	A	L	E
U	T	S	W	N	D	S	O	A	R	R	O
N	O	P	I	E	B	A	L	R	T	T	Q
A	M	B	E	R	J	A	C	K	V	B	W

Peru

The Intriguing Incas (page 133)
Answers may vary but should include some of the following information.
1. The emperor of the Incan people. Sapa Inca means *the only Inca*. He was born to the position and was not elected. He was all-powerful.
2. The government made sure the common people were cared for by making sure that they had food, clothing, and shelter. The government wanted to keep the commoners healthy because they were the common workers of the Incan Empire.
3. With terraced farming, the Incas grew crops on the steep mountain slopes. They used an irrigation system to catch the rainfall and the run-off from the snow-capped Andes mountaintops.
4. The Incas worshipped the sun god, Inti, and thought their ruler was also a god and a direct descendent of Inti. The Incas had many other gods, too, like the god of nature, the god of the moon, the god of the planets. The Incans kept statues of their gods in their homes and prayed to their gods daily. They had huge monthly festivals honoring their major gods with dancing, feasting, and sacrifice of animals (and sometimes humans!).
5. Inventions: terraced farming, freeze-dried goods, aqueducts, hanging bridges, panpipes (still very much in use today), goldsmithing, silversmithing
6. Ruins of temples, palaces, fortresses, and a royal tomb; remains of stone aqueducts; remains of terrace gardens; homes of farmers, nobles, and priests; pottery; a ceremonial pyramid called an *intihuatana* through which they communicated with their sun god
7. A young man who functioned as a mailman carrying orders and news from one end of the Incan Empire to the other. If the messages weren't accurate, the punishment was severe.
8. The system contained more than 14,000 miles of road, much of which was paved. Some sections were extremely deep with stone walls built along the edges to prevent people from tumbling off cliffs. The government owned the roads, and special permission was needed to use them (common people were not allowed on the roads). Also, the army used the roads to travel throughout the empire and stop invaders. The Incan roadrunners used them when carrying messages.
9. the Quechuas and Aymara people
10. Answers will vary.

Additional Resources

Argentina

Books

Burgan, Michael. *Argentina*. New York: Children's Press, 1999.
Explores the geography, history, culture, religion, economy, and people of Argentina.

Lourie, Peter. *Tierra Del Fuego: A Journey to the End of the Earth*. Honesdale, PA: Boyds Mill Press, 2002.
A personal look at this beautiful land at the southernmost island off the coast of South America.

Sessa, Aldo. *Gauchos*. Cologne, Germany: Konemann, 2003.
A photographic documentary of the Argentine gaucho culture.

Van Laan, Nancy. *The Magic Bean Tree: A Legend from Argentina*. Boston: Houghton-Mifflin, 1998.
A famous Argentine folk tale about the origin of the carob tree.

Brazil

Books

Berger, Melvin, and Gilda Berger. *Life in the Rainforest: Plants, Animals, and People*. Nashville, TN: Ideals Children's Books, 1994.
Covers the basic aspects of rainforest ecology, including the people who live there and the problems associated with the destruction of this area.

Cherry, Lynn. *The Great Kapok Tree*. San Diego, CA: Harcourt Children's Books, 1990.
A beautifully-illustrated story of a rainforest ecosystem and the importance of rainforest conservation.

Freland, François-Xavier, and Sophie Duffet. *Kids around the World: We Live in Brazil*. New York: Abrams Books for Young Readers, 2007.
Learn about the many different cultures and traditions in Brazil today. Spend a day with João as he wanders around Salvador de Bahia selling fitas (good luck ribbons), and take a trip with Flávia through the Amazon Rainforest.

Hollander, Malika. *Brazil: The Culture (Lands, Peoples, and Cultures)*. New York: Crabtree, 2003.
Explains the many cultural celebrations of Brazil. Special spreads throughout the book explain the origins of religious festivals and the music and dance of Brazil.

Streissguth, Thomas. *Brazil in Pictures*. Minneapolis, MN: Lerner Publications, 2002.
A beautifully-illustrated tour of Brazil in pictures.

Web Sites

The Rainforest Action Network
http://www.ran.org/
Through education, organizing, and nonviolent direct action, this organization works to protect the Earth's rainforests and support the rights of their inhabitants. Find out what you can to help save the rainforests.

The Rainforest Alliance
http://www.rainforest-alliance.org/
Learn more about the rainforest and what is being done to conserve biodiversity, transform land use practices, and raise our awareness of how we can support conservation.

Chile

Books

Dipiazza, Francesca Davis. *Chile in Pictures*. Minneapolis, MN: Twenty-First Century Books, 2007.
A beautifully-illustrated look at the land and people of Chile.

Goodnough, David. *Pablo Neruda: Nobel Prize-Winning Poet*. Springfield, NJ: Enslow Publishers, 1998.
Discusses the life and work of one of Chile's most famous writers, including his political career.

McNair, Sylvania. *Chile*. New York: Children's Press, 2000.
Explores Chile's geography, plants, animals, history, economy, language, religions, culture, sports, arts, and people.

Lourie, Peter. *Tierra Del Fuego: A Journey to the End of the Earth*. Honesdale, PA: Boyds Mills Press, 2002.
Focuses on the history of this fascinating land at the southernmost part of the world.

Shield, Charles J. *Chile*. Broomall, PA: Mason Crest Publishers, 2009.
A fresh look at the people and culture of Chile with a calendar of festivals, recipes, and ideas for reports on the country.

Underwood, Deborah. *The Easter Island Statues*. Detroit, MI: KidHaven Press, 2005.
Looks at the famous rock statues on Easter Island, what they mean, and how they got there.

Web Sites

Chile: The Official Government Site
http://www.chileangovernment.cl/
Provides a good overview of the country as well as links to other interesting sites.

Easter Island Home Page
http://www.netaxs.com/~trance/rapanui.html
Provides lots of information about the famous Easter Island and serves as a portal to many other sites, including pictures of the famous Easter Island rock art.

Embassy of Chile, Washington, DC
http://www.chile-usa.org/
Catch up on the latest cultural events and news!

Cuba

Books

Ada, Alma Flor. *Under the Royal Palms. A Childhood in Cuba*. New York: Atheneum, 1998.
The author writes about her childhood in Cuba in the 1940s. She lived comfortably and compares and contrasts the wealth and poverty in her country. Each chapter includes a specific memory or experience, with photos of the author and her family throughout.

Ancona, George. *Cuban Kids*. New York: Marshall Cavendish Children's Books, 2000.
Includes color photos of Cuban kids and their families in rural and urban settings like school, a doctor's office, a farm, at sporting events, playing music, and dancing.

Llanes, Lillian. *Havana: Then and Now*. San Diego, CA: Thunder Bay Press, 2004.
Havana was established in 1519 as a harbor city. Still a busy port, it contains many spectacular examples of Spanish colonial architecture. This book contains dozen of pictures from its past as a posh vacation spot to its current renovation.

Morrison, Marion. *Cuba (Country Insights)*. London: Wayland Publishing, 1998.
An introduction to Cuba. Looks at people in their daily lives at home, work, school, and play in urban and rural settings.

Web Sites
Cuba News Headlines. Cuba Daily News
http://www.cubaheadlines.com/
Read about what's going on in Cuba, including lots of articles about the arts, culture, people, places, and tourist destinations in the country.

Havana Times
http://www.havanatimes.org/
Billed as a Web site with "open-minded writing from Cuba," it aims to provide a balanced view of Cuba today. Interesting articles and great pictures!

iCuban.com (Three Guys from Miami)
http://icuban.com/about.html
One of the most popular Cuba sites on the Web written by three friends who want to promote Cuban culture. The writers have authored Cuban cookbooks.

Official Site of the Government of Cuba
http://www.cubagob.cu/
Includes information on the government, the people, and the history of Cuba.

Nicaragua

Books
Dall, Christopher. *Nicaragua in Pictures (Visual Geography. Second Series)*. Minneapolis, MN: Twenty-First Century Books, 2006.
A beautifully-illustrated look at Nicaragua.

Morrison, Marion. *Nicaragua (Enchantment of the World. Second Series)*. Danbury, CT: Children's Press, 2002.
Explores the history, culture, politics, and geography of Nicaragua.

Kott, Jennifer, and Kristi Streiffert. *Nicaragua (Cultures of the World)*, 2d ed. New York: Marshall Cavendish, 2005.
An engaging look at the people who call themselves Nicas. Includes maps and index. Great for research or general reading.

Web Sites
Embassy of the United States in Managua, Nicaragua
http://nicaragua.usembassy.gov/index.html
This gives good insight into just what an embassy in a foreign country does for American citizens who visit or live there.

Masaya Market
http://www.masayamarket.com/
The Web site of Masaya's famous market. This is a great place to do some "window shopping" and browse many of Nicaragua's famous handicrafts.

Vianica.com
http://www.vianica.com/
Plan your trip and find out everything you need to know to go! The beautiful photos on this site alone are worth the time it takes to access it.

Panama

Books

Augustin, Byron. *Panama (Enchantment of the World. Second Series)*. Danbury, CT: Children's Press, 2005.
Explores the geography, history, culture, industry, and people of Panama.

Henderson, Malcolm. *Don't Kill the Cow Too Quick: An Englishman's Adventures Homesteading in Panama*. Bloomington, IN: iUniverse, Inc., 2004.
The author retired to live on a group of islands off Panama's Caribbean coast. He describes his efforts to establish an organic farm and live out his dream of moving to a tropical island.

Lynette, Rachel. *The Panama Canal (Great Structures in History)*. San Diego, CA: Kidhaven, 2004.
A great way to get to know one of the world's most famous engineering wonders.

Web Sites

Panama Canal Authority
http://www.acp.gob.pa/
Check the Kids link on the home page for lots of interesting information about and photos of the Panama Canal, including how it works.

Panama Canal Museum
http://www.canalmuseum.com/
Get the story on the canal, including lots of historical photos.

Panama News: Panama's Online English Language Newspaper
http://www.thepanamanews.com/pn/v_15/issue_16/frontpage.html
Catch up on the latest news and see some great pictures!

Panama Today Magazine
http://www.panamatodaymagazine.com/
Catch up on the latest news, learn more about Panama, and plan your trip with this fun web site.

Peru

Books

Clark, Ann Nolan. *Secret of the Andes*. New York: Puffin. 1976.
A Newbery Award Book that tells the story of a young Incan boy who lives high in the mountains of Peru with an old llama herder. Unknown to the boy, he is of royal Incan ancestry.

DiConsiglio, John. *Francisco Pizarro: Destroyer of the Inca Empire*. London: Franklin Watts, 2009.
A look at Pizarro's life as a soldier and his conquest of Peru.

Landau, Elaine. *Peru*. Danbury, CT: Children's Press, 2000.
Explores the land, people, and culture of Peru.

Mann, Elizabeth. *Machu Picchu: The Story of the Amazing Inkas and Their City in the Clouds*. New York: Miyaka Press, 2007.
A beautifully-illustrated book that tells how and why Machu Picchu was built, along with the history and origin of the Incas and the destruction of their empire.

Web Sites

My Peru
http://www.myperu.org/index.html
Includes many articles about the customs and traditions of the Andean Quechua communities of Peru.

Nazca Lines and Cahuachi Culture
http://www.crystalinks.com/nazca.html
Excellent images of the Nazca Lines along with theories about why they might have been made.

The Official Tourism Site of Peru
http://www.peru.info/default.asp?leng=2
Plan your trip to Peru!

Quechua
http://www.quechua.org.uk/Eng/Main/
Learn more about the official language of the Incan Empire and one of the official languages of Peru today.

Notes